NUMEROLOGY FOR LOVERS

Richard De A'Morelli

Spectrum Ink Books

Numerology For Lovers

Copyright ©1974, 2023 Richard De A'Morelli & Spectrum Ink Books

First Edition March 1974
Second Edition July 2023

Cover image licensed from Adobe Stock Graphics. Back cover image licensed from DepositPhotos.com. Images are copyrighted by their respective owners.

All rights reserved. No part of this book may be reproduced in any form, stored in any retrieval system, or transmitted by any means, including electronic, mechanical, photocopy, recording, or otherwise without prior written permission of the publisher, except in the case of brief quotations embodied in critical reviews and certain other noncommercial uses permitted by U.S. and international copyright law. For permission requests, contact the publisher using the email address provided below.

Spectrum Ink Books
Email: Editor@Spectrum.org
Website: https://books.spectrum.org
Phone: (805) 888-2900
Fax: (805) 888-2999

Retail and wholesale orders for this title in e-book, paperback, and hardcover editions may be placed using the ISBNs below. Quantity discounts are available through our worldwide distributor, Ingram Content Group.

ISBN Numbers:
978-1-64399-057-6 : Amazon Kindle
978-1-64399-058-3 : EPUB (digital)
978-1-64399-059-0 : Retail Paperback (Amazon)
978-1-64399-060-6 : Wholesale Paperback (Ingram)
978-1-64399-061- 3 : Wholesale Hardcover (Ingram)

Number is the Word but it is not utterance.
It is wave and light, though no one sees it.
It is rhythm and music, though no one hears it.
Its variations are limitless, and yet it is immutable.
Each form of life is a particular reverberation of Number.

The Memoirs of Zeus,
Maurice Druon

Contents

ACKNOWLEDGMENTS 7

PREFACE
    Your Love Life by the Numbers 9

CHAPTER 1
    How Numerology Works 13

CHAPTER 2
    How to Construct a Love Chart 17

CHAPTER 3
    Evaluating the Love Vibration 27

CHAPTER 4
    Key to Your Romantic Destiny 53

CHAPTER 5
    Understanding the Sexual Consensus 63

CHAPTER 6
    Determining Your Karmic Liability 83

CHAPTER 7
    Guide to the Transcendent Challenge 93

CHAPTER 8
    Evaluating Your Relationships 111

CHAPTER 9
    Assessing Your Emotional Interaction 133

CHAPTER 10
    Assessing Your Sexual Interaction 153

CHAPTER 11
    Your Love Forecast 177

CHAPTER 12
    Charting Your Life Cycles 197

CHAPTER 13
    Your Love Life by the Numbers 227

ABOUT THE AUTHOR 241

Acknowledgments

This book is a new, fully updated second edition of *Numerology for Lovers*. The first edition was written in 1973 and published in the spring of 1974. It was my third book, published very early in my writing career; I was 21 at the time. Since then, I have gained volumes of knowledge about writing, editing, publishing, and today, the teeming world of self-publishing, which wasn't an option back when I was an aspiring author. It is my sincere hope that I've become a better writer since my early works fifty years ago. Regardless, I think it is appropriate to retain the Acknowledgements page from my original work since it also served as a Dedication page, and the people I thanked back then earned my gratitude then, and I remain grateful to them today. Hence, the acknowledgments below remain intact:

-o-

I cannot begin to name the many people whose influence, encouragement, and assistance over the past year enabled me to complete *Numerology for Lovers*. I wish particularly to thank my mentor, Glenn Holt, and his wife Mary; my former spiritual guide, Ronnie Hale, and her husband Claude, who took me in and saved my life when others thought I was lost; my wife, Kitty; and my good friend, Hal Daly.

I also owe a special debt of gratitude to several friends and loved ones—Sunshine, Bill Burnett, and Cindy; George Wagner, Wayne Vincent, Tom Valentine, Marcia Trotsky, Richard

Zoerink, my mother-in-law Lily Mae Schmidt, who loved me as her own son; and Gil and Carol, my downstairs neighbors who patiently tolerated my all-night typing sprees.

I wish to thank Stacy Hunt of KIIS radio in Los Angeles for her support of my work and her encouragement; Shana of KLOS radio; and the staff of two other stations, KBCA and KWST, all in Los Angeles, whose combined influence and superb programming set the ideal mood for writing this book.

Thank you one and all!

—Richard De A'Morelli,
Los Angeles, California
January 16, 1973

Preface
Your Love Life by the Numbers

This book is about numerology and your love life. If you have never experienced a meaningful relationship, numerology can help you attain this wonderful experience. If you are in love now, the science of numbers can help to ensure your ultimate happiness. Or, if your relationships always seem to fall apart for no apparent reason, this book might explain why and help you to improve your future romantic prospects.

Happiness in love does not develop accidentally. Any successful relationship incorporates three basic qualities. First, you must recognize your own needs and desires. Only then can you determine the type of relationship that would be ideal for you. Second, you must learn to understand your mate's virtues, flaws, inhibitions, and deepest cravings. You can then use these insights to evaluate your complementary and contrasting characteristics in terms of compatibility. Lastly, cooperative interaction should flourish if you expect your relationship to afford any real emotional or sexual fulfillment.

These qualities—self-awareness, mutual awareness, and cooperative interaction—comprise the framework of a harmonious relationship and perfect love. Without them, involvement would lack constructive stimulation and durability. In other words, you and your mate would be miserable for the time, probably brief, you remain together.

How can we achieve genuine self-awareness? How can we detect and analyze a partner's nuances? And how can we determine our compatibility with a potential lover in advance?

One way to gain these insights is quite costly: psychoanalysis. Another approach involves calculated risk—fall in love and try to work things out as time passes. Unfortunately, both options have serious drawbacks and may accomplish more harm than good for both individuals. There is, however, a third alternative: the science of numbers, practically applied.

Numerology eliminates both the expense of psychotherapy and the risk of taking the dive and finding out the hard way that it was a mistake. With the information provided in this book, you can master and begin applying numerology in just a few days, or even hours. The only mathematical skill that you'll need is the ability to count up to 22. With very little effort, you'll be able to construct a complete "love chart" for yourself as well as others. You'll discover ways to identify compatible mates at a glance, pinpoint the major pitfalls in your relationships, and secure a lifetime of happiness in romance and marriage.

Numerology for Lovers is a practical guide to finding the perfect mate and cultivating the ideal love affair—and making it endure. Using the tables and interpretive charts given in these pages, you can navigate a hassle-free and gratifying course through the emotional wilderness.

For those who are interested in acquiring a deeper understanding of this practical science, the text will also:

1. Present a unique and accurate system for plotting highly detailed love charts, examining romantic trends, personality traits, and life cycles, and analyzing other data pertinent to emotional and sexual intimacy, complete with step-by-step instructions and examples.

2. Explain the nuances of sexual interaction using insights gleaned from numerology, and reveal how these trends can help ensure successful and gratifying relationships.

3. Unveil a practical system for translating number trends into behavioral patterns. With the insights provided in this book, you'll be able to transcend the complexities of human analysis and acquire a clear, concise method for calculating and accurately interpreting a love chart quickly and easily.

Anyone can master the techniques presented in this book. The years of study, the intricate calculations and painstaking research typically required to master the more complex aspects of numerology, have been replaced by a simplified method that is both accurate and valuable. Once you have mastered a few basic techniques, the love charts you create will provide the same remarkable insights that celebrity numerologists charge significant amounts to provide.

Emotional, physical, and spiritual interaction between romantic partners doesn't need to be a complicated, painful experience. The practical science of numerology can reveal a clear-cut path to ultimate happiness in love and marriage.

Chapter 1
How Numerology Works

*I*n numerology, we believe that every human being, young and old, in every walk of life and every part of the world, is influenced by universal energies that ebb and flow predictably. These "universal vibrations" play a crucial role in our lives from the moment of birth, shaping our personalities, strengths and weaknesses, attitudes, and beliefs. As adults, these powerful but natural currents affect every facet of our day-to-day existence including our career choices, health, friendships, and romantic involvements.

People react to universal vibrations in unique ways. As we become adept at crafting and analyzing numerology charts for ourselves and others, the intricacies of these energies and their effects will become obvious. We'll begin to see why certain days are more productive than others, and why our endeavors and relationships sometimes erupt into chaos. We will understand why we think and behave as we do under various conditions—and we'll discover practical ways to improve ourselves.

Numerology satisfies three important prerequisites. It discloses the significance of ever-changing vibrations in our daily affairs, reveals when a particular trend is increasing or decreasing, and advises us in our quest for success and happiness. You don't need a deep knowledge of numerology's theoretical principles to apply the practical methods outlined in this book. You need only to understand that these vibrations exist, and their influence on our lives is remarkably strong.

By definition, Numerology is the study of numbers and their significance in your life. But the numbers alone have no real impact on your life, your surroundings, or your future. For the sake of convenience, numerologists assign numbers to differentiate one vibration from another. It is more convenient, for example, to refer to the "3 vibration" than to use a string of adjectives to describe the characteristics and effects of that vibration each time we refer to it. So, to describe the vibration of individuality, exploration, and innovation, we merely refer to the "1 vibration" and its properties are understood.

The appearance of certain numbers or combinations of numbers in a numerology chart reflects the trends influencing our lives and affairs at any given moment. By interpreting these number patterns, we can glean a host of useful insights into ourselves and others. This is true in every facet of life, including romance. Desires, ambitions, needs, habits, weaknesses, sexual attitudes and responses, and many other innate qualities that we inherit at birth become obvious at a glance.

Early numerologists based their science on nine primary vibrations, represented by the digits 1 through 9. They believed these vibrations, called "primary vibrations," are responsible for shaping an individual's personality and destiny. Today, the foundation of modern numerology is based on these same vibrations, but some additional numbers are now used—five in particular. Called "karmic vibrations," or "master vibrations," they are represented by the numbers 11, 14, 16, 19, and 22. These vibrations have special meanings which we'll explore later in this book, and their appearance in a numerology chart denotes unique trends or circumstances that do not occur under any of the nine primary vibrations.

When applying numerology to matters of romance, we are particularly concerned with four key aspects of a person's love chart. Each provides valuable insights that can be utilized for self-improvement and to attain a happy and satisfying love life. These four aspects are Love Vibration, Romantic Destiny, Sexual Consensus, and Karma.

The Love Vibration reflects a person's emotional desires, attitudes, habits, strengths and weaknesses, and day-to-day behavior within the framework of an intimate relationship. It can also be used to evaluate a current or potential romantic partner in the same way. With this information, we can delve beyond surface appearances and discover what an individual is really like, how they think, act, feel, desire, and fear, and what they want most in an intimate relationship.

The second aspect, Romantic Destiny, reflects future trends in your romances, and the road you are traveling in life. It broadly reveals the experiences that lie ahead and provides an overview of your romantic prospects as you go through life. Trends affecting love, marriage, divorce, new relationships, travel, adventure, and major life changes can be examined here.

The third aspect, Sexual Consensus, examines a person's physical cravings, attitudes, behaviors, and habits. This aspect also reveals inhibitions, desires, insecurities, and motivations within the context of physical intimacy.

The fourth aspect, Karma, reflects a person's subconscious behavior, pitfalls, and life lessons, and reveals ways to perhaps overcome key challenges that may lie ahead on the road of life.

Various other aspects must also be carefully examined and interpreted in a numerology love chart, using similar methods. Past, present, and future love and sex cycles can be discerned, and relationship comparisons performed quickly and easily.

As we begin this fascinating journey into the Science of Numbers, it's important to remember that, in numerology, vibrations are natural energies, neither good nor bad. For the most part, they are neutral until we react to them. Some may seem more challenging to deal with than others, but all can be transformed into positive or negative influences by our choices and actions in daily life. Each vibration has unique significance. How you respond, whether you seize promising opportunities or allow yourself to be impacted in less favorable ways, ultimately depends on you.

Numerology does not provide a crystal ball, and it's not a supernatural cure-all. Indeed, there's nothing supernatural about it. Numerology does not promise a foolproof solution to every problem. But it can provide a series of cosmic signposts that we can heed or ignore. It can reveal the intricate workings of universal trends and how they affect our day-to-day affairs. In a sense, it is a mirror of human nature, a roadmap charting our spiritual destiny, and a schematic of the wider universe.

Read on to discover how numerology can provide valuable glimpses into yourself, others, and the world around you!

Chapter 2
How to Construct a Love Chart

Numerology, with its myriad practical applications, gives rise to various types of charts. The "Personal Profile" chart, for instance, zeroes in on character analysis, while the "Love Chart" brings matters of romance, marriage, and physical intimacy into focus. This type of chart can divulge a remarkably accurate profile of an individual's character traits, attributes and shortcomings, fears, desires, and attitudes. It can shine a light on conscious and subconscious behavior patterns in intimacy and other facets of daily living. A plethora of useful insights on how to identify physically and emotionally compatible partners, and how to forge enduring relationships can also be discerned, as well as an understanding of how life cycles and personal day, month, and year trends can shape how we think, feel, and react in our day-to-day affairs.

A blank Numerology Love Chart appears on the following page, and three additional blank charts are included at the end of this book, which you can detach or photocopy. This template enables you to record numerological data as you work through the steps of crafting a chart. You could use a blank sheet of paper if you prefer, but the template offers a convenient way to create numerology love charts for yourself, your partner, a potential mate, and anyone else. The layout of the chart makes it easy to enter data for two people, make intricate comparisons, and jot down notes as you progress. Step-by-step instructions for getting started are provided in this chapter.

NUMEROLOGY LOVE CHART

Your Birth Name	Partner's Birth Name

Birthdate (xx/xx/xxxx)	Birthdate (xx/xx/xxxx)

Major Aspect	You	Mate	Notes
Love Vibration			
Romantic Destiny			
Sexual Consensus			
Karmic Lessons			
Challenge			

Life Cycles	You	Mate	Notes
Cycle 1 (0-9)			
Cycle 2 (10-18)			
Cycle 3 (19-27)			
Cycle 4 (28-36)			
Cycle 5 (37-45)			
Cycle 6 (46-54)			
Cycle 7 (55-63)			
Cycle 8 (64-72)			
Cycle 9 (73+)			

To construct a numerology love chart, you must know your full name at birth and your date of birth. Always use the exact name and spelling on your birth certificate. The one exception to this rule is if your name or spelling changed before your second birthday, and you grew up using this new name, then you should use that for your numerology chart.

To include your partner or a prospective mate in the chart, you'll need their full name at birth and date of birth as well. Disregard name changes due to marriage or adoption unless the "before age two" exception discussed above applies. Make sure you have the correct information for both yourself and your partner, as the accuracy of your chart depends on it.

Follow the instructions given below, and soon, you will be utilizing numerology with the precision of a professional. If you want to interpret each step as you progress, review the appropriate chapter for an interpretation after you've completed each calculation; then, return here and continue on to the next step. Alternatively, if you would rather finish all the calculations before interpreting the results, simply work through the steps, and then look up the interpretations for each vibration

Step #1: Determining the Love Vibration

Your *Love Vibration* is determined by the vowels in your full name at birth. Each vowel corresponds to a numerical value listed in this Conversion Table:

1	2	3	4	5	6	7	8	9
A	B	C	D	E	F	G	H	I
J	K	L	M	N	O	P	Q	R
S	T	U	V	W	X	Y	Z	

Every syllable in the first, middle, and last name should have at least one vowel. In English, the vowels are A, E, I, O, U, and sometimes Y, as we'll discuss in a moment. All other letters are consonants.

When is "Y" a vowel? Here's the rule: treat "Y" as a vowel if it is the *only* vowel in a syllable. For example, it is a vowel in

Mary, Tyler, and Dorothy because, as shown in the examples below, "y" (in bold) is the only possible vowel in the syllable.

Mar-**y**
T**y**-ler
Dor-o-th**y**

However, in these next three names, "y" is not a vowel—it's a consonant—because the syllable in which it appears has a vowel (shown in bold) other than "y":

Ca-s**e**y
Ash-l**e**y
W**a**yn**e**

Very rarely, a first or middle name won't have a vowel. This can happen when a child is given a name such as JJ. In this case, the vowel total for that name would be 0 (zero), and you go on to calculate the remaining parts of the name as explained below.

Now that you can recognize the vowels in your name, write your full birth name on a piece of paper. Using the Conversion Table on the previous page, write the number value of each vowel directly below the letter as we've done in the example below. Some numerologists circle or underline the vowels to set them off from the consonants and then assign the values.

```
J E N N I F E R    L Y N N    M A R S H A L L
  5     9   5        7          1       1
```

Add the vowel numbers in the first name, and then reduce that sum to a single digit (1–9). By "reduce," we mean add the digits in the resulting sum together. In our example, Jennifer's first name has three vowels with values of 5 + 9 + 5. So we sum these digits, and the total is 19. Now, we reduce to a single digit by adding together the 1 and 9 from the total: 1 + 9 = 10. Reduce again to a single digit: 1 + 0 = 1.

Familiarize yourself with this technique because it will be used for various calculations in this book. When you're directed to "reduce to a primary vibration" (meaning a single digit between 1 and 9), this is how it's done.

There's a second "reducing" technique used in this book, where you'll be instructed to "reduce to a primary or a master vibration." There are five "master vibrations" with special significance, and they are 11, 14, 16, 19, or 22. So to do this, you follow the procedure described above but reduce a number until it is either a single digit or one of the five master vibrations.

Returning to the task of deducing your Love Vibration, add and then reduce the vowels in your middle name. Then, do the same for your last name.

Using our example, Jennifer's middle name has one vowel, and its value is 7. It is already a single digit, so no need to reduce it. Make a note of that sum. Then do the same for Jennifer's last name. It has two vowels; each has a value of 1. So, 1 + 1 = 2. It's a single digit, so we write down that total.

For the last step of this calculation, add the three name totals together: first name (1), middle name (7), last name (2).

$1 + 7 + 2 = 10$

And then we reduce. Here, we use the second rule, reducing the sum of the first, middle, and last name to either a primary vibration (1-9) or a master vibration (11, 14, 16, 19, and 22):

$1 + 7 + 2 = 10 \mid 1 + 0 = \underline{\mathbf{1}}$

This tells us Jennifer's Love Vibration is 1.

Use this formula to calculate your Love Vibration, and then do the same for your partner or a potential mate. To understand the results, refer to the interpretations in Chapter 3.

Always, *always,* verify that you have correctly identified the vowels and consonants in a name and converted the letters to the correct numerical values. Also, double-check your math. One small error can result in major inaccuracies in a chart.

Step #2: Determining the Romantic Destiny

The second aspect to consider in a numerology love chart is the *Romantic Destiny* vibration. It is derived from your birth day, month, and year.

MONTH CONVERSION KEY

January: 1	July: 7
February: 2	August: 8
March: 3	September: 9
April: 4	October: 1
May: 5	November: 2
June: 6	December: 3

Write down your birthdate, and use the Month Conversion Key above to translate your birth month to a single digit. Reduce your birth day to a single digit. Do the same for your birth year.

Add the three single-digit values together (day + month + year), and reduce the sum to a primary vibration (1-9) or a master vibration (11, 14, 16, 19, and 22).

Here's an example, using Jennifer Lynn Marshall's birthdate of August 16, 1955:

Month: **8**
Day: 1+6 =**7**
Year: 1+9+5+5=20 | 2+0=**2**

Add the reduced day, month, and year sums:

8+7+2=17 | 1+7=**8**

This calculation affirms that Jennifer's Romantic Destiny resonates with the 8 vibration.

Use this procedure to determine your own Romantic Destiny, and do the same for your partner or a potential mate. To understand the meanings of the Romantic Destiny vibrations, refer to the interpretations in Chapter 4.

Step #3: Determining the Sexual Consensus

The third major aspect in your numerology love chart is the *Sexual Consensus*. This is derived from all the vowels and consonants in your full birth name. To start, write down your full name again. Use the Conversion Table given earlier to assign the correct number values to each letter in your name, placing the digits directly below the letters.

Next, add the numbers in your first name and reduce to a single digit. Do the same for your middle name, and then your last name. Add the three resulting sums together, and reduce to a primary vibration (1-9) or master vibration (11, 14, 16, 19, or 22). Here's an example:

```
J E N N I F E R    L Y N N    M A R S H A L L
1 5 5 5 9 6 5 9    3 7 5 5    4 1 9 1 8 1 3 3

First Name:
1 + 5 + 5 + 5 + 9 + 6 + 5 + 9 = 4 5
4 + 5 = 9

Middle Name:
3 + 7 + 5 + 5 = 2 0
2 + 0 = 2

Last Name:
4 + 1 + 9 + 1 + 8 + 1 + 3 + 3 = 3 0
3 + 0 = 3
```

Adding the three sums for the Jennifer's first, middle, and last name gives us 9 + 2 + 3 = 14. As 14 is a karmic vibration, we do not reduce it any further.

Determine the Sexual Consensus vibration for yourself and your partner or a potential mate, and refer to Chapter 5 to interpret the results.

Step #4: Determining the Karmic Liability

The fourth aspect of a love chart involves identifying your *Karmic Liability*. Some numerologists use the term "karmic lessons" and describe these as life experiences or challenges an individual must learn or overcome in daily living. Others regard this aspect as a reflection of subconscious behavior.

To determine your Karmic Liability, examine all the numbers in your full name (from Step #3), and look to see if any primary numbers between 1 and 9 are missing. The absence of a primary vibration in your name indicates a karmic lesson or subconscious challenge that needs to be overcome. If not addressed, it could negatively impact your romantic pursuits and other aspects of your life.

Again using Jennifer's name as an example:

```
J E N N I F E R   L Y N N   M A R S H A L L
1 5 5 5 9 6 5 9   3 7 5 5   4 1 9 1 8 1 3 3
```

On close inspection, we find that the only missing number in Jennifer's name is 2. This means her Karmic Liability, or karmic lesson, is represented by the 2 vibration. If more than one number is absent, it indicates multiple karmic lessons must be addressed.

Rarely, all nine primary digits will be present in a name, reflecting that the individual has no karmic lessons. In this case, write a "0" in the Karmic Liability section of the chart.

Follow this procedure to determine the Karmic Liability for yourself and your partner or a potential mate. Refer to Chapter 6 for an interpretation of your karmic lessons.

Step #5: Determining the Transcendent Challenge

The *Transcendent Challenge* is the fifth major aspect of a numerology love chart. This reflects your ideal mode of self-expression in intimate relations. To calculate this aspect, use your date of birth. Write down the fully reduced day, month, and year sums from Step #2. For example, Jennifer's birthdate—August 16, 1955—sums to 8 for the month, 7 for the day, and 2 for the year.

Add the *day* and *month* sums together and reduce the result to a primary vibration (1-9) or master vibration (11, 14, 16, 19, 22). Write down the result.

Next, add the *month* and *year* sums together and reduce the result to either a primary or master vibration.

Lastly, add the two sums you obtained from these steps and reduce the result to a primary vibration (1-9), or a master vibration (11, 14, 16, 19, and 22) to discover your Transcendent Challenge vibration.

Continuing our example, Jennifer's Transcendent Challenge vibration is 6, and this is how we arrived at that:

Transcendent Challenge Diagram

8 7 2

6 9

6

Use this method to discover your Transcendent Challenge vibration, and then do the same for your partner or a potential mate. Refer to Chapter 7 to interpret the results.

Step #6: Creating Your Love Chart

Whenever you craft a numerology chart, you should jot down the results for future reference so you don't have to repeat the process. For convenient reference, you can record your results in a blank love chart. As previously noted, three copies of this template are provided at the back of this book, and you can record your data there or make photocopies of the chart for your use.

The next five chapters delve into interpreting the major aspects of your love chart covered in this chapter. For an even deeper understanding of numerology, read further to learn about other advanced operations in the remaining chapters of this book. These techniques and guidelines will yield valuable insights you can use to evaluate your romantic relationships, assess your compatibility with potential partners, and cultivate the ideal romantic relationship. You'll also learn about how you can infuse more passion, depth, and meaning into an existing romance, how to chart and interpret life cycles and personal trends, and how to mend a relationship teetering on the brink of a breakdown.

As you work through this book, you will likely discover that the numerology love charts you compile for yourself and others are strikingly accurate. However, if a chart doesn't resonate with your personality, ensure that your calculations are correct and double-check the spelling of the names used. A minor error can drastically impact the accuracy of a numerology chart.

Chapter 3
Evaluating the Love Vibration

1

The 1 vibration reflects individuality, change, renewal, and a fresh approach to the problems of daily life. It is the vibration of the idealist, explorer, and trendsetter. The native with this Love Vibration is assertive, ambitious, and highly opinionated, imbued with a quick mind and a keen sense of humor. These individuals are active, fun-loving, attracted to the new and the unusual, and always searching for provocative, untried life experiences. They refuse to be bound by convention and insist on running their personal lives as they see fit. Independent and proud, they do not like to be criticized, and they resent interference from friends and relatives. Both genders hold unconventional views on love and marriage. Their relationships are often unique and progressive.

ROMANTIC CONSENSUS

MALE

This man is an ardent, resourceful partner. He is a staunch advocate of contemporary ideas and has few inhibitions. He enjoys challenges and often takes risks in daily living. When he comes up short in love, and he often does, he demonstrates amazing resilience, passing quickly on to new, more provocative involvements. Although an excellent judge of character, he is attracted to flighty, unstable mates. He rarely procrastinates and may instantly profess his affection for an attractive partner, plunging headlong into a deep relationship. Despite being prone to recklessness, he usually manages to avoid tragic mishaps; but when he does suffer a train wreck in a relationship, it's likely to be monumental. This individual can derive great pleasure from the most unlikely love affairs. Freedom is essential to his well-being, and he refuses to be dominated by an aggressive partner.

FEMALE

Outgoing, adventuresome, and sophisticated, this woman has a wide range of interests in everything and loves life. She is sensuous and affectionate, open-minded, and liberal. She is prepared to try anything once but quickly learns from mistakes. She is deeply aware of her partner's needs and strives to please, realizing that her own happiness will be increased as a result.

This woman refuses to be controlled by a lover. She will not forfeit her identity or circle of friends to appease a jealous, possessive mate. She abhors the prospect of being stereotyped as a drab housewife and may pose an impossible challenge for the man who holds the old-fashioned notion that a woman's place is in the home. She knows that her life promises more. Only the most exceptional partner can keep her happy in a love affair or marriage.

Open relationships and honesty appeal to this woman. She must feel deep respect for a lover before she will commit herself. She should never be mistaken for the submissive type: She's dynamic, knows how to get her way, and will quickly burst a headstrong partner's ego if forced into an unhappy relationship.

2

These individuals are generous, patient, tactful, and kind. They are good listeners, loyal confidants, and sympathetic counselors, imbued with a fine sense of justice and high morals.

They prefer stability and roots to constant change, as the latter upsets their inner balance. They tend to avoid aimless flirtation and seek to establish deep, lasting attachments.

Both genders ruled by the 2 Love Vibration are sociable and fun-loving, but they need occasional solitude. They tend to shun offbeat or unconventional lifestyles. They're not especially ambitious and often wait for others to take the initiative, especially in romance. Trustworthy and dependable, they can shoulder enormous responsibility on sudden notice if called upon to do so. They detest arguments, preferring to yield, even when they know they are right, and they work to quickly calm trouble waters and reconcile opposing factions.

ROMANTIC CONSENSUS

MALE

This conscientious mate is loyal and steadfast, a born romantic, brimming with optimism, and imbued with a kind disposition. He may seem passive, but he is definitely not a pushover. He possesses incredible fortitude and courage which become evident when the need arises. He is not egotistical and won't flaunt his virtues to impress a prospective mate. He may shy away from great displays of emotion, yet he is capable of deep intensity once aroused by a partner who knows how to bring out his best qualities.

The 2-male is patient and adaptable, capable of succeeding in romance or marriage under the most difficult conditions. His aversion to divorce reflects a desire for roots and security. This attitude may motivate him to persist in a relationship long after others would have given up and walked away.

FEMALE

Affectionate, devoted, and sensitive, this woman is often too trusting, and she may be easily offended by a partner's thoughtless words or deeds. She may appear naive and vulnerable, but she's more worldly and determined than she appears. Insecurity is a major pitfall for her, and she may worry too much about failing in a romance or marriage. She is also concerned about what others think and may suffer along in an unhappy relationship so that her friends or family won't think less of her.

When this individual accentuates her positive attributes, she is imaginative, gentle, and sympathetic, usually easy to get along with, but prone to occasional moods and sentimentality. She instinctively knows her partner's needs and desires, and she strives eagerly to please. She suffers from deep inhibitions, yet she is adept at helping a partner overcome their hang-ups and shortcomings. She is happiest when she has no connection to the business world and is free to lead a comfortable, sheltered life revolving around family and friends.

3

Beauty and creativity are highlighted under the 3 Love Vibration. Most of these individuals are highly creative and talented. Expressive, eloquent, and soulful, they are capable of being particularly successful in the fields of music, writing, art, or theater. Creative endeavors are compatible with their vibrant personalities. They find it difficult to submit to routine, abhor boredom, and resent taking orders.

These individuals must be constantly active, mingling with diverse and exotic people, exploring every facet of life, even the mundane. They find the hidden beauty in all things and want to share their feelings with others, expressing a dramatic quality in every thought and action.

ROMANTIC CONSENSUS

MALE

Open-minded, gregarious, and direct, this man has an enthusiastic approach to life. He is highly intelligent and imbued with a complex but fascinating personality. As a lover, he is liberal, fun-loving, and progressive, refusing to be bound by conventional norms or societal expectations. Permanent attachments typically don't appeal to him; but matched with the right partner, his love can be incredibly deep and enduring. At times, he is difficult to please as he expects a lover to conform to his lofty ideals.

Strange and exotic lifestyles fascinate this man, causing him to gravitate towards unconventional relationships. While typically loyal, he wants and needs his freedom, especially in sexual relationships. He does not equate extramarital trysts with infidelity and thus may indulge in occasional illicit affairs. He tends to be quite candid and expects his mate to be equally straightforward. His knack for making a current lover feel genuinely appreciated contributes to his appeal and promotes mutual gratification.

FEMALE

Radiant and sensuous, this woman is adventurous, daring, fun-loving, and drawn to the strange and the exotic. She is imaginative, highly creative, and sometimes rather eccentric. Her romances are in a constant state of flux or turmoil, and she enjoys exciting new twists in her affairs. She is discriminating in her choice of lovers and may come across as rude when she ignores overtures from would-be partners who don't interest her. She demands much from a mate, but once united with a lover deserving of her devotion, she commits herself fully.

This woman is not particularly inhibited, but she may have peculiar hang-ups about intimacy. She places high importance on her physical appearance, and she goes to great lengths to maintain and enhance her beauty. Although prone to jealousy and possessiveness, she dislikes those qualities in a partner. Freedom is essential to her happiness, and she may end a relationship if she feels her identity or freedom is in jeopardy.

This woman enjoys honest, wholesome relationships based on mutual trust and admiration, infused with a spicy sex life. She expects her partner to be entirely candid, even though she is sensitive and easily hurt. Her spontaneity, charm, and sparkling personality make her popular and sought after.

4

Individuals governed by the 4 Love Vibration have an organized, systematic approach to daily living. They are stable, proud, and reliable, imbued with a strong will and common sense. In romance, they are typically cautious. They form commitments gradually, building their relationships on a solid and sensible foundation. Once involved, they are capable of steadfast devotion.

These individuals are caring, unpretentious, and honest—sometimes too honest, leaving their partners with hurt feelings. They avoid flamboyant gestures to win popularity. Although they can adapt to change when required, they prefer the familiar and resist change, sometimes fiercely, until a compelling reason for it becomes clear. Their practical outlook is very evident in their romances. They dislike flighty, promiscuous people and shun people they perceive as phony, superficial, or immoral. They tend to avoid brief, torrid affairs in favor of meaningful long-term relationships.

ROMANTIC CONSENSUS

MALE

Loyal and steadfast, this man is gifted with a great sense of humor and admirable self-control. He recognizes shortcomings in his partner but is tolerant of their flaws, and he can be highly empathic. He tries hard not to impose impossible standards. Healthy love relationships appeal to him, but he does not crave love and can function well in daily life without it. He wants but does not require companionship and intimacy. He will likely have many professional and leisure interests to distract his attention from romance until the right person comes into his life.

As a mate, this individual tries hard to please. But he does not understand the opposite sex particularly well. In fact, he may find it challenging to understand women who are flighty or temperamental, which can occasionally lead to frustration.

Jealousy and possessiveness are characteristic of this man, and these qualities are occasionally responsible for romantic strife. He recognizes his shortcomings but finds it difficult to change, and he might never succeed in doing so. His patience and generosity are commendable and make up for his other shortcomings.

FEMALE

The woman governed by the 4 Love Vibration is sensible, down-to-earth, and very emotional. At the same time, she is quite stable and secure, always viewing her love life objectively. She is a considerate, trusting companion, strong-willed and reliable. Possessiveness is one of her habits that she tries to overcome but with only limited success. She does not hesitate to speak her mind, even when it hurts the feelings of others. Although she does not typically express her deeper emotions overtly, she can be very demonstrative with the right partner.

The 4-female can be incredibly stubborn. She is inclined to dominate in a domestic environment and needs a strong male to reinforce her equilibrium. As a lover, she is generous, patient, and loyal. She appreciates the beauty of physical contact but practices moderation in love and sex. She does not usually suffer from inferiority or low self-esteem, but she enjoys praise and expects it from those who profess to love her. Once she receives a compliment, she makes a special effort to repeat the same actions to earn more of the same. Less inhibited than the 4-male, she knows how to relax and have a good time.

5

Sexuality, freedom, and adventure are highlighted under the 5 Love Vibration, and its natives have an eager, curious approach to life. They are fascinated by strange and exotic people, places, and lifestyles. Fiery, assertive, and straightforward, they possess great physical magnetism and a strong sex drive. Deeply attuned to the foibles of human nature, they instinctively know how to prod, tease, stimulate, and intrigue a desired mate. Sex is an important part of their relationships, and physical affection is essential to their happiness. While these individuals don't always use good judgment or common sense, they rarely mope over disappointments. They are slow to learn from mistakes and may repeat the same errors over and over. Their romantic pursuits frequently erupt into chaos, yet they never cease trying to mix love with adventure.

ROMANTIC CONSENSUS

MALE

Courageous, energetic, and outspoken, this man makes a stimulating companion. He is a good conversationalist and a convincing promoter or salesperson, especially where his own personality is concerned. He is, at times, the "great pretender," and is prone to inflating his importance to prospective lovers. He tends to shy away from responsibilities and commitments at every opportunity, enjoys frequent change, and must be forever active, enjoying every exciting experience life offers.

An intense and imaginative lover, this man can be overly critical and temperamental; but most of the time, he is easy to get along with. He craves intimate companionship but his methods for attracting partners and obtaining fulfillment may not always be realistic. Rarely, 5-males can be unethical or dishonest, particularly when they encounter resistance to getting what they want.

This man loves deeply, yet he may struggle to remain with one partner for long periods. He may marry several times before finding a comfortable niche. Flattery is one of his weaknesses, and a perceptive mate will quickly realize that he responds well to praise as well as physical affection.

FEMALE

The woman influenced by this Love Vibration is deeply sensuous, inquisitive, and brimming with rare enthusiasm. She has an insatiable appetite for offbeat life experiences. She is an ardent, demonstrative lover, willing to impulsively commit herself completely, but just as inclined to walk away from a relationship if her partner does not live up to her lofty and sometimes unrealistic expectations.

Independent and proud, this woman refuses to be limited by convention, and she lives by deep and often unconventional convictions. Her romances are based on modern, progressive ideals, reflecting her temperament as a fun-loving individualist. She wants honesty and trust in her relationships and abhors the prospect of being too dependent on her mate.

This woman's love life may not be particularly stable. Change, adventure, and short-term romances are typical under the 5 Love Vibration. Interesting new twists must be present in this woman's romances or she will lose interest and drift away. She does not want to be trapped in a monotonous existence, particularly with a headstrong partner who encroaches on her freedom or tries to control her.

6

Love and security are crucial to individuals governed by the 6 Love Vibration. They crave companionship. Affection, both physical and emotional, is essential to their happiness. They may often give the impression that they can function well without love, but that is rarely true. Because they have complex personalities and succumb to frequent mood changes, they are not always easy to understand or live with.

These individuals crave love, yet they are not very stable in romance. They may change their minds about what they want suddenly and without warning. Moody or illogical behavior, especially among women under this vibration, may frustrate their partners. A deep-rooted inferiority complex is common under the 6 Love Vibration, and these individuals may provoke romantic discord by worrying that the happiness they seek in love is undeserved or will be short-lived. Once they acquire confidence and an improved self-image, the gentle, affectionate nature of this vibration will shine through, making them ideal partners in love and marriage.

ROMANTIC CONSENSUS

MALE

This individual is strong but inclined to be rather passive in romance. He holds many deep convictions, including some that may strike his partners as old-fashioned. He is not averse to marriage but will not sacrifice his identity to appease a jealous or overbearing spouse. Though typically a conformist, he can be open-minded in his approach to love and marriage when persuaded by an understanding woman.

A male governed by the 6 Love Vibration does not usually impose rigid standards, but he can be old-fashioned when it comes to behavior and morals. He expects his mate to remain loyal and devoted, and to avoid illicit flings and scandals. He shuns potential lovers who express masculine tendencies, and he dislikes the idea of men and women competing. He treats his spouse as an equal but usually likes to occupy the driver's seat.

In love and marriage, this man is not especially open or communicative, and he can be difficult to understand. At times, he may seem aloof and preoccupied. Despite his affectionate nature, his quick temper may sometimes lead to tension. He loves deeply yet often fails to express his true feelings. He can be easily hurt by a lover's thoughtless words or actions, and he does not easily forgive past slights. His generosity, patience, and sensitivity are most evident when his feet are planted firmly on the ground.

FEMALE

This woman is gentle, kind, and demonstrative. Her approach to romance and marriage may be unconventional, yet in other areas of life, she is a devout conformist. She goes through regular stages of trying to acquire a more glamorous image and struggles to overcome her inhibitions. Yet, she never quite manages to discard her embrace of tradition. She has a deep sense of morality, and there's no confusion in her mind between right and wrong. She places a premium on home and family. It is difficult for her to have sex without love, and she has an idealistic view of romance, seeking emotional and sexual intimacy within the framework of a serious relationship that she expects will inevitably lead to marriage.

Although fickle and impulsive at times, this woman often battles insecurities. She needs a demonstrative partner who showers her with affection to convince her of his devotion. She is prone to upset easily when criticized by a mate, and although she may look calm and poised, she has a short fuse and a fiery temper that she tries to suppress with limited success.

In love, this individual is yielding, open to new ideas, and eager to please her partner, even to her own detriment. She falls in and out of love easily, but she is discriminating in her choice of partners for the most part. She wants a strong, dependable mate with whom she can share her feelings, her dreams and goals, and her life. She admires masculinity, but over-muscled jocks are a turn-off for her. She admires determination, courage, and inner strength.

7

The 7 Love Vibration is associated with analytical thinking, self-awareness, and spirituality. Although it favors romance and marriage, it can create instability in romantic affairs. Those who resonate with the 7 approach love sensibility and with a sense of realism, although this sometimes makes them seem cool or aloof. They are blessed with sharp, analytical minds, and may dissect and scrutinize issues from every angle before reaching conclusions or taking action. Their propensity to ask "Why?" can test the patience of close friends and partners, and may cause strain in relationships. Often, they overthink things and may be perceived as hypercritical of others, especially their romantic partners.

ROMANTIC CONSENSUS

MALE

The man under the 7 Love Vibration is observant, intuitive, but also grounded, outspoken, and sometimes overly blunt or hypercritical. He holds firmly to his convictions and lives by his principles but rarely tries to sway the opinions of others. He tends to adopt a passive stance in love, and while generally patient, he can become obstinate when criticized by a partner, sometimes defending an opinion that he knows is flawed. Navigating the complexities of love can be challenging for him, and intense emotions may unsettle him. Consequently, he keeps a tight rein on his heart and generally avoids taking risks in love.

This man may harbor intense sexual desires and can, on occasion, become consumed by physical gratification, although he typically suppresses these urges, sometimes even denying his true feelings. He is hesitant to commit to a serious relationship unless he is confident of his ability to adapt to the necessary changes. Despite his pragmatic and cautious nature, an extraordinary partner who understands his apprehensions and weaknesses may stir his emotions, leading him to become a passionate and devoted lover.

FEMALE

The woman resonating with the 7 Love Vibration seeks a relationship grounded in reality and built on a foundation of mutual trust. Having experienced painful relationships in the past, she is cautious and fickle. She depends on common sense and refrains from rushing into a committed relationship without meticulously weighing the pros and cons. This overly analytical nature may discourage potential suitors, and if she spends too much time procrastinating, valuable relationship opportunities might slip away.

This woman is highly sensitive and yearns for love. Yet, she often retreats into a protective shell, which can be challenging for a partner to penetrate. Although she projects an image of practicality and stability, she isn't as grounded as she seems. A deep-seated sense of inferiority can emerge unexpectedly.

In romance, she strives for balance and practicality. She often scrutinizes her partner's actions, searching for underlying intentions. Seeking to fully understand a partner's motivations, she patiently probes until she uncovers the truth. This can make her appear calculating, and her pursuit of understanding may come across as overly critical or demanding. She sets high standards for her partner and expects him to align with her ideals. In sexual relations, she achieves physical satisfaction easily and does not struggle for it. She values honesty and transparency in relationships and requires a high degree of personal freedom.

8

The 8 Love Vibration in numerology is synonymous with business acumen, leadership, and power. It is not typically viewed as highly emotional, but this doesn't mean that those influenced by the 8 can't find happiness in love. Symbolizing confidence, generosity, prosperity, and determination, this earthy and materialistic vibration is linked with a robust drive to excel in all endeavors. In romance, these individuals often play the dominant role, expecting their word to be final. They are drawn to adventure and change, provided that they offer constructive outcomes aligning with their life goals. Challenges energize them, and they relish a stimulating debate, although their temper may flare if their views are discredited, or they feel belittled.

Both genders prefer sensible, grounded relationships. They are put off by extreme emotional reactions as well as jealousy and possessiveness. Their perspective on love and sex is conventional, perhaps even a bit old-fashioned. However, they might experiment with alternative lifestyles if inspired to do so by an exceptional partner. These individuals value privacy immensely, require their own space, and dislike intrusions from relatives or friends.

ROMANTIC CONSENSUS

MALE

Assertive, dynamic, and confident, this strong-willed man knows his life objectives and the routes to achieve them. He relishes overcoming opposition in business and romance, assured of his ultimate triumph. He is drawn to healthy, stable love affairs but can manage day-to-day life without love, as he doesn't consider it essential for personal fulfillment. Focused on his goals and ambitions, he refuses to be bogged down by emotional predicaments. He easily moves on from overbearing relationships or those that inhibit his style, never dwelling on past missteps, and he uses setbacks as motivation to redouble his efforts.

In romance, this man is patient and determined. He is committed to providing his partner with material comfort, emotional support, and sexual satisfaction. However, while he is passionate, be can sometimes be inconsiderate or selfish during sex. He doesn't usually exhibit overt affection, and sentimental dates or places may elude his memory, leading to hurt feelings in his partner.

FEMALE

The woman with an 8 Love Vibration is devoted and down-to-earth in romantic affairs, yet she can be quite passionate with the right person. She is generous and fun-loving, giving freely of her emotions without losing balance. She recognizes that love is a give-and-take proposition. She tries to avoid impulsive decisions, preferring to thoroughly understand a partner before committing her heart or entering a serious relationship.

While a purely domestic life centered on home and family likely won't satisfy her, she possesses a broad range of interests and goals to distract her from domestic concerns. Nevertheless, she is adaptable and can excel in the role of a diligent homemaker, devoted wife, and nurturing mother with the right partner. She is willing to make significant sacrifices without complaint when passionately in love.

In romantic relationships, this woman is considerate, affectionate, proud, and direct, but also compassionate and gentle. She tolerates a partner's faults to an extent, but she will not endure a weak or indecisive partner. She seeks meaningful companionship, not an emotional burden. If a partner falls short of her expectations, she takes the initiative to suggest improvements. If these suggestions go unheeded, she will move on to a more grounded companion.

9

The 9 Love Vibration reflects a profound, sensitive, and introspective temperament. Those influenced by this vibration are discreet, trustworthy, and idealistic. They can occasionally be fickle, yet they are usually accepting of a partner's faults. As they are deeply emotional, they may lack stability in romance. These individuals are prone to poor judgment in selecting a partner, despite their preference for honesty and transparency. While capable of deception when the need is sufficiently compelling, they generally strive for sincerity.

Individuals under the 9 vibration love passionately and intensely. However, they are hypersensitive and can be quick to take offense at a partner's thoughtless words or actions. They fear rejection and are uneasy about rejecting a potential mate's advances, even when they know that the person cannot meet their idealistic standards. These individuals require roots and security for happiness. They need praise and affection to express their best qualities. While impulsiveness isn't typically associated with this Love Vibration, a deep fear of loneliness may lead to impulsive actions and mistakes. They make ideal partners for empathetic mates who can help them develop inner fortitude and stability.

ROMANTIC CONSENSUS

MALE

Men influenced by the 9 Love Vibration usually aren't aggressive or flamboyant. They possess personal magnetism and charm, and their remarkable depth and sensitivity compensate for any shortcomings. Their approach to the opposite sex is warm but cautious and somewhat reserved. Their true feelings for a prospective lover may not always be apparent, leading to missed opportunities in romance. These individuals exhibit inner strength and compassion in their relationships. However, beneath their calm exterior, they often harbor self-doubt. Many of these men are sentimental romantics, frequently entwined in a complex web of hopes and fears about their romantic fate.

The 9-male is perceptive and highly attuned to a partner's needs and desires. He's typically loyal but may hesitate to form long-term commitments. He is an idealist, searching for the perfect love relationship. Fear of loneliness and poverty are his greatest challenges. He craves privacy, solitude, and personal space, yet fears that his mate may emotionally withdraw or leave abruptly. Deep-rooted insecurities may cause him to dwell on romantic disappointments. When a love affair fails, he typically attributes it to his own inadequacies or mistakes.

FEMALE

The 9-female deeply values love and companionship. However, she may be acutely insecure, which can make her overly dependent on loved ones. She worries excessively about failing as a lover, often neglecting to focus on overcoming her insecurities. Prone to impulsiveness, her choice of partners may be less than ideal. Despite being highly responsive, she may appear aloof and distant. Her tendency to brood about the past can lead to frequent mood swings and bouts of depression.

In love, this woman can be a deeply sensuous partner, brimming with emotions, hopes, and dreams. However, she requires an exceptionally patient and understanding mate to unlock her positive attributes. She thrives in deep, honest relationships based on mutual trust and respect, appealing to her idealistic nature. She derives intense pleasure from satisfying her mate. She strives eagerly to please, often ignoring her own needs and sacrificing too much for her mate.

11

Individuals influenced by the 11 Love Vibration view romance as the most beautiful life experience possible. They are not content with ordinary love affairs—they seek relationships that are deep, inspiring, ethereal, and soul-stirring. They are capable of forming genuinely platonic friendships as well, and they often remain in the good graces of former lovers, building lifelong friendships with some of them.

Talented, inquisitive, insightful, and often psychically gifted, natives of this Love Vibration can be exciting and tireless lovers under the right circumstances. At times, however, they may seem aloof; other times, they fluctuate between extremes of affection, leaving their partners uncertain of how they truly feel. They are capable of intense devotion but tend to idolize their partners and overlook their glaring faults. Consequently, they can fall out of love abruptly if a partner's imperfections become too apparent.

Many individuals governed by the 11 Love Vibration tend to fondly reminisce about past relationships, idealizing their partners, exaggerating how happy they were (even if they weren't all that happy), and making present relationships challenging due to unrealistically high expectations.

ROMANTIC CONSENSUS

MALE

Men under the 11 Love Vibration handle life's daily ups and downs efficiently but may be fickle, moody, and unpredictable in love. They can appear distant to potential lovers unless they are truly enamored. Born romantics, they are dreamers and perfectionists, highly creative and quite talented in the realm of dramatic expression, particularly writing and music. They crave the excitement of romance and rely on a lover's companionship for security and inspiration. They are straightforward and opinionated, but rarely domineering.

In romance, the 11-male is empathic, encouraging, and supportive. He is patient and very perceptive but sometimes lacks tact, blurting out thoughts before thinking. This can lead to hurt feelings and failed relationships. This individual has high standards, and few partners can hold his attention for long. He admires goal-oriented individuals, though his emotions often override his judgment. His aura of mystery and penchant for secrecy often result in a long string of love affairs before he finally settles down.

FEMALE

The woman who responds to the 11 Love Vibration is generally more grounded than her male counterpart. Although she may have dark moods and insecurities, and she often makes hasty decisions, her self-control allows her to circumvent precarious situations for the most part, and she is adept at extricating herself from difficult relationships when she's had enough. She sets high standards for a lover and won't settle for anything less. A prospective mate must earn her respect and admiration before she will consider a commitment. However, she's not against casual flings when someone attractive crosses her path. She gravitates to partners who are witty, intelligent, outgoing, bold, dynamic, and responsible. Flighty, promiscuous lovers do not appeal to her, although some of her former lovers may accuse her of precisely that behavior. She goes out of her way to avoid prejudiced, narrow-minded, and negative people.

In love and marriage, the 11-female is passionate, and she enjoys giving and receiving physical affection. Though she may appear aloof at times, her love, once given, is deep and true. Once she commits to a mate, her attention is unlikely to stray. However, this woman is deeply sensitive and easily offended by thoughtless words or a lover's forgetfulness of sentimental dates. If she feels that a partner has intentionally slighted her, she may strike back and is quite capable of holding a grudge.

This woman revels in her femininity, but she refuses to be docile or submissive. A partner who disrespects or takes her for granted will quickly understand her disappointment, and she may not be quick to forgive. She will end a relationship abruptly if her mate becomes overbearing or abusive. However, for the partner who respects her depth and sensitivity, she will prove to be a fun-loving, devoted, and affectionate companion.

14

Individuals attuned to the 14 Love Vibration are fiery, passionate, fun-loving, outspoken, and open-minded. They typically have a great sense of humor and an innate magnetism. Their natural curiosity compels them to explore every life experience, and they want to try everything at least once. They do not usually attach themselves to any one person or group but are constantly on the go, meeting new people and savoring every life experience that comes their way. The strange, offbeat, and exotic hold a special attraction for them. These individuals love challenges and often dive headfirst into situations without considering the repercussions. They struggle to learn from past experience and tend to repeat the same mistakes, stubbornly refusing to accept that things won't turn out as they would like.

ROMANTIC CONSENSUS

MALE

Men governed by the 14 Love Vibration refuse to accept the notion that their lives are controlled by fate. They want to be in full command of their destiny at all times. They live by the credo that all is fair in love and war, pursuing their desired mate and relying on their dynamic personality and magnetism to gain their affection.

These individuals have a strong sex drive, and physical intimacy is imperative in their relationships. They enjoy a vibrant social life and an adventurous lifestyle, basking in popularity from a wide circle of friends. They often overexert or scatter their energy, pursuing too many diverse goals at once, pushing themselves to the brink.

As a lover, this man is daring and determined, but he is often unpredictable. He prefers to avoid commitments and domestic responsibilities. He often confuses love with physical pleasure, sometimes to his partner's detriment, and he may jump into an affair purely for pleasure without considering the consequences. Marriage may not suit this individual until later in life, if then. He has too many ambitions that divert his attention from home and family.

FEMALE

Women attuned to the 14 Love Vibration are independent, fun-loving, and deeply sensuous. They are intrigued by unconventional and exotic lifestyles. Their natural curiosity often leads them into unexpected predicaments, and impulsiveness can result in heartbreak and disrupted relationships. Their romantic engagements are intense, stimulating, and unique, but typically brief. They often confuse love with sex, leading to complications in their relationships.

As a lover, the 14-female is extravagantly affectionate. She is open-minded and values her freedom. A controlling partner will quickly discover that this woman is owned by no one, and she won't be pressured into a commitment. She is not especially candid and will hold back her thoughts to avoid potential conflicts. However, when she falls in love, it's intense and potentially obsessive. Although she despises jealous, possessive partners, she might become one herself if she senses her partner's affections wavering. She may not admit the true depth of her feelings for a mate, which may confuse those who think she views them as nothing more than a fling.

The 14-woman responds well to praise and flattery, but she is also selective and attaches great importance to her partner's physical appearance. This selectiveness may sometimes be misconstrued as snobbish. Her strong intuition allows her to sense her partner's vulnerabilities, which she may occasionally use to inspire her lover or bring levity to the relationship. She fiercely rejects the idea of being controlled. If a partner takes her for granted, she can turn off her feelings as swiftly as one might switch off a lamp.

16

The 16 Love Vibration presents significant challenges for those in pursuit of a harmonious love affair or marriage. This master vibration is associated with "emotional crucifixion" in numerology, often linked to separation, divorce, and illicit affairs. However, these pitfalls are merely signposts on the road of life, and individuals have the freedom to choose their paths.

Individuals ruled by the 16 Love Vibration are intensely emotional and sexual. Prone to bouts of depression, their mood swings and hypersensitive temperament may lead to impulsive commitments and abrupt transitions between romantic relationships. Intense and passionate, they deeply commit themselves on impulse but may just as quickly move on and rush into a new romance. This can subject their love life to frequent upsets and short-lived affairs. Their romances may fall apart inexplicably, and even those that endure might seem unsatisfactory. The common denominator in these tumultuous relationships can usually be blamed on their fluctuating moods and expectations.

These individuals are gifted with creativity, imagination, and intuition. They often foresee prescient glimpses of the future, but acting impulsively on these visions as they often do can lead to mistakes and chaos. Both genders can experience deep love and devotion, often demonstrating an instinctive understanding of their partners' needs.

Natives of the 16 Love Vibration typically struggle with inhibitions and insecurities. They tend to attract unsuitable lovers, losers, and grifters, especially before the age of 35. As they mature, their understanding of their needs and desires matures too, leading to better romantic prospects. They would benefit by cultivating confidence, stability, better control of their moods, and realistic expectations in love.

ROMANTIC CONSENSUS

Men and women who resonate with the 16 Love Vibration are dreamers, romantics, and quite sentimental. They are prone to mood swings and sudden infatuations. They often dwell on past mistakes and may attempt to shield themselves from future disappointments. Impressionable, dramatic, and creative, they make stimulating but unstable partners. At times, they may appear distant or secretive. With their complex personalities, they can be hard to understand or analyze.

These individuals seek an intense, gratifying relationship that sparks their passions and transcends the ordinary. Most eventually learn to appreciate the peace and stability of a harmonious romance or marriage, particularly after turning 35. They usually focus their thoughts and daily activities around their current mates, and they feel deep anguish when a romance fails. Many successful actors, writers, and painters share the 16 Love Vibration, which accentuates creativity and dramatic self-expression. It is the most challenging vibration to navigate but holds the greatest promise of happiness and fulfillment for those who find what they seek in a partner and life.

19

Individuals governed by the 19 Love Vibration exhibit a dynamic blend of the 1's initiating and independence-seeking qualities, and the 9's finishing, compassionate, humanitarian characteristics. They are self-reliant and confident with a strong desire to stand out from the crowd, combined with a deep understanding and appreciation of life's experiences. They bring together the explorative and the reflective, marking them as initiators who are also capable of bringing things to a fitting conclusion.

The 19 Love Vibration instills a yearning for freedom and independence but also an intense longing for love and companionship. These individuals cherish their personal space and autonomy, yet they can simultaneously give and receive love with an intensity that is both beautiful and overwhelming. Their approach to romance and sex is nuanced; they seek partners who respect their individuality and freedom but are also ready and willing to share in their deep emotional world.

ROMANTIC CONSENSUS

MALE

The man attuned to the 19 Love Vibration is adventurous, ambitious, and driven. He often seeks a partner who can match his energy and passion, yet he also appreciates a lover who can provide a calming influence in his life. This individual seeks love and companionship but values his independence. He is often the initiator in romantic pursuits, but he also knows when to step back and allow a relationship to naturally unfold.

The 19-male has a strong desire for personal achievement and often strives to be the best partner he can be. However, he needs to guard against becoming too focused on his goals and forgetting his partner's needs. When in love, he can be caring, passionate, and generous. He values honesty and expects the same from his partner. If he feels his independence is threatened, he may retreat, but if he is given the space he needs, he can be a loyal, committed, and loving partner.

FEMALE

The woman who resonates with the 19 Love Vibration is strong and independent, yet sensitive, deeply compassionate, and understanding. She values her freedom and typically seeks a partner who understands and respects her need for personal space. At the same time, she craves deep connections and is not afraid to dive into the emotional depths of a relationship.

She is adventurous and likes to explore new experiences, often bringing a fresh perspective to her relationships. Yet, she can also be reflective and introspective, frequently relying on her past experiences to guide her future actions. When in love, she is attentive, caring, and committed. She can be intense and passionate, but she also knows when to give her partner space. If her partner respects her need for independence and shares in her deep emotional world, she can be a dedicated, loving, and supportive companion.

22

Those influenced by the 22 Love Vibration are dependable, resourceful, grounded, and loyal. They are imbued with a strong will and a practical approach to life's daily problems. They may not exude sensuality or flamboyance, but their loyalty, courage, and problem-solving skills are impressive. They want stability and harmony in every aspect of their lives, and they approach romance with realism. While capable of intense emotion, these individuals are reserved and not particularly demonstrative. They are too grounded and practical to succumb to impulsive desires. They avoid promiscuity and scandal, instead seeking balanced, meaningful relationships that promise lasting value.

ROMANTIC CONSENSUS

MALE

The man influenced by the 22 Love Vibration values romance and companionship yet maintains his independence. He doesn't pursue intimacy recklessly, understanding that life and love unfold in their own time. If love and marriage aren't feasible at a particular life stage, he will prioritize other constructive pursuits. When in a committed relationship, he is confident, discreet, and trustworthy. He avoids gambling with feelings—his own or others—and he will quickly extricate himself from any situation tainted by scandal. Although he may not be inherently assertive, he is filled with determination and displays adaptability and resilience during crises. He thrives within conventional norms, and exotic or unconventional lifestyles do not appeal to him. Although his enthusiasm might not be fiery, he is a steadfast, honest, and conscientious lover.

FEMALE

The woman attuned to the 22 Love Vibration seldom dives impulsively into love affairs. She is a pragmatic, down-to-earth realist with formidable self-control. She is not easily deceived or led astray, and she's a superb judge of character, especially in romance. She cautiously weighs the merits of a relationship, opting for gradual commitment. Her romances are built on a solid foundation, and she is averse to moody, insecure people, drifters, and losers. She admires a partner who has clearly defined goals and a strong willingness to work diligently towards achieving them.

As a mate, this woman is devoted, honest, reliable, and self-sufficient. She keeps her emotions in check, avoiding dramatic or troubled individuals. She guards against becoming too dependent on her mate and expects her partner to be self-reliant too. Confident in her self-worth, she does not feel the need to seek affection and reassurance from brief love affairs. She can engage in sexual intimacy without forming deep attachments, but she typically finds encounters based solely on sexual attraction to be superficial and unfulfilling.

The 22-woman's devotion to a deserving partner, and her close friends, is unwavering. She is discerning in her choice of friends and lovers, preferring to wait for an ideal relationship to develop naturally than rush into a messy affair. She usually steers clear of casual relationships, knowing such encounters may offer less than they cost in the long run.

Chapter 4
Key to Your Romantic Destiny

1

*M*any sudden and unexpected changes will come your way under the 1 Romantic Destiny. You will find happiness in love, but also more than your share of disappointments. Wrong decisions, impulsiveness, procrastination, or failure to act when opportunities arise, are usually to blame.

Colorful, stimulating, and creative partners are in your future, and you will share many adventures and unforgettable memories with romantic companions. Be careful, however, to avoid interactions that could lead to scandal. Discretion isn't always one of your strong points, but you need to develop it, or your natural curiosity and desire to experience the new and the unusual could lead to regrets and painful consequences. Don't expect your first intense romance to succeed; you will have many relationships with a wide variety of partners before you find your match and settle down. As long as you remain confident and optimistic in the face of disappointment, your romantic prospects will be many and rewarding. Don't worry when one relationship ends because another is just around the corner. You won't ever be lacking meaningful companionship.

2

The 2 Romantic Destiny promises a stable, harmonious love life. You'll inevitably experience disappointments as lovers come and go but for the most part, you will be immune to serious loss and upheaval. Your problems will never be insurmountable, and conflicts always seem to resolve in your favor. The benevolent 2 vibration promotes happiness in love, stable home life, and tranquility. As long as other numerological vibrations in your love chart are relatively benign, it is highly likely that you'll achieve ultimate fulfillment in romance.

The one caveat to keep in mind is that you must be careful to avoid entanglements with partners who clearly don't deserve you, and those with abusive or addictive personalities. These individuals will find it easy to play on your sympathies and take advantage of you or abuse you. Poor judgment is a peril associated with the 2 Romantic Destiny. To avoid this pitfall, always be selective and settle only for the best when choosing a spouse as well as in your friendships.

3

The 3 Romantic Destiny often brings great success and recognition, especially for those who pursue creative endeavors, particularly, music, acting, art, and writing. However, your love life may not be as fulfilling as you'd like. Under the 3's intensely creative vibration, mood swings are common and occasional bouts of depression. At times, you may feel that happiness in love seems distant, even unattainable. Many people with this Romantic Destiny go through the first half of their lives having intense but brief relationships that lack substance and leave more unhappy memories than happy ones. Guard against a tendency to impose idealistic standards and expectations on yourself and others, or you may set yourself up for heartache. The 3 vibration also instills a tendency for impulsive behavior and poor judgment, which could lead you into troubled waters.

Until you understand that a "perfect" soul mate does not exist, you may find yourself flitting from one relationship to another. Many individuals with the 3 Romantic Destiny have several stormy marriages before they finally adjust their expectations and settle down into a fulfilling long-term relationship.

4

The 4 Romantic Destiny favors practical, earthy romances. You'll likely have ample opportunities for travel and adventure, and a restless urge to explore everything the world has to offer. You may be tempted to dive into exotic love affairs or secretive trysts. Although some people may find gratification in such encounters, they typically don't lead to positive outcomes under the 4 and thus should be avoided. Your greatest opportunity for happiness in love will likely come with someone you've known for a long time, and it will develop gradually within the framework of a down-to-earth and stable relationship.

Once you have committed to a long-term relationship, you'll be the stabilizing influence. You will find yourself placed in situations where a calm, sane, sensible approach is required to maintain domestic harmony. Your willingness to cope with these situations without complaint will be a key factor in the stability and longevity of your relationship. By keeping your feet planted firmly on the ground and willingly shouldering your share of responsibilities or more, your desire for enduring romantic bliss will be realized.

5

Life under the 5 Romantic Destiny will be exciting, fast-paced, and free of boredom and routine. Most individuals who share this destiny trend fall in and out of love many times before settling down in a long-term commitment. You will be drawn to attractive, passionate partners, and they will have a significant effect on your life outlook as well as the course of your life. You may have a strong urge to seek out the new and the unusual, but you should guard against reckless behavior and poor judgment, as these are the principal pitfalls of the 5 Romantic Destiny, and you could lose more than you expect.

Your earlier years will be punctuated by many sudden and unexpected changes, some welcome, others not. After age 32, your life will stabilize and you'll find your stride. You will likely lead a colorful or unusual existence and could find yourself pursuing an alternative lifestyle. You enjoy being different, shocking people, and taking the path in life no one expects.

The 5 destiny trend may occasionally foreshadow health disorders, an increased risk of accidents, and rarely, problems arising from over-indulgence or addiction, two pitfalls of the 5 that must be avoided. Be especially cautious around machinery, and avoid risky occupations and contact sports.

6

Depending on the other vibrations present in your chart, this Romantic Destiny can be a mixed bag. It can promote romantic discord and strife, or great happiness. A careful examination of the other components in your chart will help to clarify which trends may be prevalent and suggest the best path you can follow to achieve a gratifying love life. The 6 vibration symbolizes domestic responsibility, marriage, and home life. You'll have many opportunities to establish deep emotional attachments with lovers and platonic friends. Some individuals who resonate with the 6 vibration marry at an early age. However, your choice of lovers may be questionable, and if you aren't careful, romance could turn into a painful ordeal for you. In later life, when you've learned to be discriminating and to choose your romantic companions based on more than looks or sex appeal, you will find your path to ultimate happiness in love.

Family and home life will play a significant role in your day-to-day existence. Under this destiny vibration, your best chance for achieving romantic fulfillment will revolve around your friends and people you've known for many years. Children will also make a notable contribution to your happiness. Be wary of jealous relatives, as this destiny trend foreshadows that family members may interfere in your personal affairs or attempt to control your life. Remain firm in your convictions, and you'll rise above the potential fallout from their meddling. Avoid illicit flings, which could have painful consequences.

7

Wisdom and spirituality are accentuated under the 7 Romantic Destiny. Throughout life, you'll be called upon to develop a deep understanding of human nature, and this will bring you a wide circle of friends and popularity. Unfortunately, you don't always apply these insights to your relationships, and your romances may prove discouraging. The 7 destiny trend does not particularly favor love or marriage, although you can find happiness if you are willing to devote yourself to the task and work hard at it. You may have a string of short-term romances, but few will provide much fulfillment. Too often, you are drawn to unstable or abusive partners. The potential pitfalls of this Romantic Destiny trend can be overcome by cultivating self-confidence and being more selective in your choice of partners. Steer clear from those who do not have your best interests at heart, and your opportunity for happiness in love will greatly improve.

8

Your romantic journey will be vibrant and fulfilling, though peppered with sudden twists and turns. The 8 Romantic Destiny favors material and emotional success. Throughout your life, you'll find yourself in control of your surroundings and your future. Like most people, you'll make your share of mistakes, but they will never be so serious that they can't be rectified swiftly and with minimal trouble. Early marriage may tempt you, but the ensuing relationship may not live up to your expectations. If negative influences appear in other aspects of your numerology chart, this mistake could lead to a tumultuous, unsatisfying love life for some time.

Travel is often in the cards under the 8 destiny trend, and you will likely take numerous trips, both for business and pleasure. You will be able to forge many wonderful memories in your travels with your family and loved ones.

9

Under this Romantic Destiny vibration, your love life could be challenging. The 9 sometimes forewarns of fragmented relationships and marital strife. Happiness may seem elusive at times, even unachievable. You may be thrust repeatedly into situations that require spur-of-the-moment decisions. Through perseverance and inner strength, you'll be able to overcome the hurdles of this destiny trend and forge a satisfying love life.

Throughout your life journey, you will often find yourself extending your kindness and generosity to friends, family, and even mere acquaintances. You'll shoulder your loved ones' concerns without complaint and navigate challenging scenarios that will be a rich source of insights into the complexities of human nature.

On the bright side, the potential pitfalls and challenges of this destiny trend can be overcome and turned into constructive energy. You'll be given many opportunities to utilize your past experiences and apply what you've learned. Cultivating good judgment and maintaining an optimistic perspective will pave the way for an ideal romance to blossom, leading to lasting happiness.

11

Under the 11 Romantic Destiny vibration, your life will be filled with unusual and thrilling adventures. Your romances will be dynamic and invigorating, some may even be inspired, and none will bog down in boring routine. Although some of your love affairs may lack stability, you'll find joy in writing the most unlikely, offbeat, and unconventional love stories. You will have opportunities to interact with glamorous partners who can do much to enrich your life, but you must guard against scandal. The 11 destiny trend can foreshadow illicit affairs and unsavory involvements, leading to heartbreak or loss of reputation. Given the unpredictable nature of romances under this vibration, self-restraint, discretion, and good judgment will be key to securing your prospects for gratification and long-term happiness. You may marry multiple times due to your fascination with partners who are not necessarily compatible with you, but you'll never be short of adoring companionship. Your complex but intriguing personality, high intelligence, and diverse talents will enhance your appeal to potential partners throughout your life.

14

The 14 Destiny Trend foretells a life brimming with adventure and change. Boredom should never be a problem for you. Whenever tedium looms, you'll find yourself immersed in novel situations, grappling with fresh challenges. Frequent travel is likely, but so is a predisposition to chronic health issues and accidents, so it's important to take precautions in daily living to maintain your health and well-being. Extravagance, over-indulgence, and risky behavior should be kept in check.

Your love life may be punctuated by an extended series of alluring but short-lived relationships. Meaningful interaction might be hard to find at times. You may struggle to differentiate between love and physical attraction, leading to discord and occasional chaos in romantic pursuits. Although you are capable of passionate responses, your love affairs sometimes may seem one-sided and transient. Once you've connected with a partner who complements your temperament, you'll be able to establish a relationship that will be fulfilling and long-lasting.

Under the 14, women should take extra precautions to prevent unintended pregnancies. Men should steer clear of risky behavior and unnecessary hazards involving chemicals, machinery, and large bodies of water.

16

With your Romantic Destiny attuned to the 16 vibration, your prospects for happiness may be challenging. Heartache may be no stranger, and you might struggle through more than your share of unsatisfying relationships. A tendency to blur the line between love and physical attraction could lead to a string of brief but stormy affairs with attractive but emotionally incompatible partners. A few individuals under the 16 destiny trend may become entangled in abusive relationships. Love affairs that start on a promising note may dissolve without apparent reason. Fortunately, such dire outcomes are preventable. Numerology reveals the trends at work in your life from moment to moment and enables you to use this knowledge to your advantage. Thus, it is always possible to turn lemons into lemonade and downpours into rainbows.

To mitigate the potential pitfalls of the 16 destiny trend, examine the other aspects of your numerology chart—your Love Vibration, Sexual Consensus, Karmic Liabilities, and Life Cycles, discussed in Chapter 12. Use these insights to pinpoint the source of challenging conditions in your life and take steps to mitigate them. Focus on cultivating your attributes, managing your shortcomings, and developing a plan to circumvent potential pitfalls. With determination and self-awareness, the 16 destiny trend, though daunting, can be transformed into a positive force. Your sensitivity and deep emotions inherited from the 16 vibration can thus be turned into benefits that work for you rather than against you.

19

Under the 19 Romantic Destiny, your prospects for love and marriage hold boundless possibilities. Many opportunities to form meaningful relationships will arise throughout your life. You will be in full control of your affairs and hold the reins of your destiny. Should you fall short of your aspirations or fail to achieve happiness in love, the responsibility will rest solely with you. Remember that your greatest adversary is often yourself.

Adventure, sudden change, new experiences, and travel typically accompany this destiny vibration. Financial prosperity and social prominence are favored as well. Your capacity and willingness to make sound decisions and execute plans at the opportune time will play a significant role in determining how far you climb up the ladder of success, both in material affairs and romance. Your errors, when you make them, are rarely minor, and bad decisions can lead to upheaval. Tap into your maturity to distinguish right from wrong as you navigate through life's daily challenges. The 19 master vibration will test your ability to wield power fairly and compassionately. Exercise good judgment and common sense, and make the right choices to ensure the right outcomes.

22

Under the 22 Romantic Destiny, if happiness often seems elusive, it's likely because you are standing in the way of your own progress. Your love life will improve when you learn to go with the flow and adopt an open-minded, flexible approach to intimacy. You'll be given many opportunities to forge stable, satisfying relationships, but it will be up to you to seize these chances and lay the groundwork to achieve enduring love.

The 22 vibration doesn't usually favor early marriage. Resist the temptation to rush into a commitment until you are confident of your maturity to handle a reciprocal relationship. Your best shot at finding romantic fulfillment lies with a practical, down-to-earth partner with whom you share mutual trust and respect. It might be someone you've known for a long time. Under the 22 destiny trend, timing is key, and you must have the wisdom and self-restraint to let your relationships blossom naturally. Like an exquisite wine that gets better with time, your prospects for romantic fulfillment will flourish when you give love time to grow.

Chapter 5
Understanding the Sexual Consensus

Sexual intimacy is intrinsic to the allure and beauty of romance. It is the physical bond that unites lovers, not just in a biological sense, but on emotional and spiritual levels as well. When physical intimacy is dysfunctional, it can swiftly destroy a romance or marriage, even among mature, well-adjusted partners.

In the 1960s, the Sexual Revolution ushered in a wave of moral freedom, gender equality, and broad departures from tradition. Yet, sixty years later, men and women still struggle to understand and interact with one another. Despite newfound equality and freedom, they have little understanding of sex within the context of male-female interaction. In simple terms, most people appreciate the erotic pleasure of sex but overlook the emotional and spiritual components of lovemaking.

This chapter aims to address this lack of understanding, providing you with useful insights into the dynamics of your sexual interaction with your partner, and a set of numerological tools you can use to assess your level of physical intimacy and compatibility with your mate. The interpretations provided in these pages address practical yet relevant inquiries put forth by individuals in love relationships and may likewise apply to your relationship:

- Am I sexually passive or an assertive initiator?
- How does my sexual performance compare?

- Am I sexually inhibited and, if so, how and why?
- What type of partners am I sexually compatible with?
- What are my shortcomings in physical intimacy?
- How does my partner respond in a sexual context?

In numerology, these questions are answered by taking a close look at the Sexual Consensus vibration. This is the third major aspect of a love chart, and it is broken down into five areas: Motivation, Response, Inhibitions, Compatible Partners, and Possible Shortcomings.

When analyzing the Sexual Consensus vibration, be aware that it does not necessarily reflect an individual's thoughts or behavior at a particular moment. Instead, this crucial aspect throws light on a person's sexual potential. It can reflect your predictable attitudes and behavior under given circumstances. With these insights, we are better able to refine our intimate responses, overcome potential shortcomings and pitfalls, and help our partners discover their best selves, bolstering our prospects for mutual satisfaction in physical intimacy.

Using the interpretive guidelines below, let numerology reveal the concealed meanings of your own and your partner's Sexual Consensus vibration.

1

MOTIVATION: Dominant; assertive. Those influenced by the 1 Sexual Consensus are dynamic leaders, explorers, and trendsetters who are approach relationships enthusiastically. They confidently assume the initiative, integrating fresh and innovative practices into their relationships. They are the ones to make the first move to attract a potential lover's attention, persisting with tenacity and not giving up easily.

RESPONSE: Exceptional. Males are easily stimulated, generous in their affections, and possess a strong sex drive. They instinctively sense a partner's preferences and dislikes.

Females are sensuous, elegant, passionate partners in sex who are highly responsive and can achieve orgasmic bliss repeatedly and with little effort. Both genders are imaginative: Their erotic fantasies play a strategic role in their sexual relationships. They are attracted to the unique and unusual. Prolonged foreplay adds to their pleasure and encourages them to be more mindful of their partner's needs.

INHIBITIONS: Most individuals who resonate with the 1 Sexual Consensus do not have significant hang-ups in sex. Their perspective on morality is liberal, and they form their own judgments on right and wrong. Some lack self-confidence and thus may shun experimentation, but most are open-minded and willing to explore stimulating lovemaking techniques. A few of these women may worry excessively about unintended pregnancies.

COMPATIBLE PARTNERS: Sensuous and demonstrative partners with a curious and eager approach to sex are the ideal match for these individuals. Lovers who are bold, confident, open-minded, and reliable are most compatible with these natives. Flighty, selfish individuals, and those who become highly emotional during physical intimacy are ill-suited to this temperament. Serious, practical lovers who strictly adhere to conventional norms may find little common ground with a partner governed by the 1 vibration and should seek intimacy elsewhere.

POSSIBLE SHORTCOMINGS: Selfishness and a tendency to rush through the sex act, often resulting from an overly eager approach to lovemaking, are the main pitfalls of the 1. Some natives seek orgasmic release at their partners' expense. This behavior is counter-productive: neither partner is apt to derive satisfaction from the ensuing relationship. Strong curiosity is another inherent risk of the 1 vibration that must be controlled (but not eliminated entirely) to avoid self-damaging forms of experimentation.

2

MOTIVATION: Generally passive. Natives of the 2 Sexual Consensus don't typically exhibit aggressive qualities. However, they have a strong sense of morality and can be quite stubborn when forced into uncomfortable situations or pressured into sexual encounters. Otherwise, these individuals are cheerful, cooperative, and go with the flow.

RESPONSE: Variable. In relationships based primarily on physical attraction, these natives don't respond well. They steer clear of exotic lovemaking techniques and may show a lack of enthusiasm during the sex act itself. However, when an emotional connection is present, they can become passionate and demonstrative. They often equate love with sex and seek both in their relationships. Given the right circumstances, they can be adaptable, cooperative, and eager to please, often foregoing their own pleasure to satisfy their mate.

INHIBITIONS: Shyness and lack of confidence or self-esteem are common among individuals who resonate with the 2 Sexual Consensus. They may be reluctant to experiment with unfamiliar activities or positions because they don't want to fail or look foolish to a lover. Fortunately, their inhibitions aren't insurmountable. Patient and understanding mates can help them overcome their fears and explore new dimensions of uninhibited sexual expression.

COMPATIBLE PARTNERS: Thrill-seekers and those who desire erotic pleasure without emotional commitment should be strictly avoided. These individuals seek and need a sex mate who is also a love mate. Strong, devoted partners imbued with sensitivity, imagination, and a sense of moderation are good matches for these men and women. They respond favorably to a sensitive approach to lovemaking, and they aren't compatible with forceful, extremist personalities.

POSSIBLE SHORTCOMINGS: A lack of determination and inner fortitude are possible pitfalls under the 2 vibration. These gentle, caring partners often give more than they receive, and some endure abusive relationships because they don't stand up for themselves out of fear that they may lose a lover's affection. Some are deeply emotional in bed, and this may impede their sexual fulfillment at times. They need to cultivate willpower and self-confidence to achieve greater enjoyment in sex and love.

3

MOTIVATION: Assertive. Those who resonate with the 3 vibration are imaginative, open-minded, and fun-loving. They express themselves dramatically in thought and action and often make the first move to initiate physical intimacy. Clever, bold, and persistent, these high-enthusiasm individuals rarely give up. In love and sex, they almost always achieve what they desire.

RESPONSE: Outstanding. Both males and females are easily aroused and capable of intense passion. They respond well to physical stimuli and appreciate unusual techniques during foreplay. They enjoy the beauty of male-female intimacy, often using sex as a medium of communication and expressing deep feelings through physical contact. They desire, but don't insist on, an emotional component in their relationships. They are capable of maintaining a purely sexual affair for the sake of physical pleasure.

INHIBITIONS: Some of these individuals may suffer from minor hang-ups, but no serious inhibitions are indicated under the 3 vibration. Most are honest, open-minded, and express sexuality freely without moral or psychological restrictions.

COMPATIBLE PARTNERS: Assertive, gregarious, and preferably creative partners who enjoy physical intimacy and approach lovemaking with an open mind interact well with this temperament. Adventure, change, and novel experiences must be included in the ideal love affair. Mates stuck in a rut or prone to emotional outbursts are incompatible, as are those who limit their lovemaking to the ordinary or perceive sex as a necessary but dull chore. Natives of the 3 vibration typically derive great pleasure from oral sex, and similarly inclined partners are most apt to enjoy mutual fulfillment.

POSSIBLE SHORTCOMINGS: A gullible or impressionable nature is the main pitfall here. Individuals who resonate with the 3 Sexual Consensus can be easily led astray by undesirable partners and may sometimes stumble into scandals. A few might become preoccupied with physical gratification and engage in reckless pleasure-seeking. Rarely, exhibitionism and a fascination for cheap thrills may surface, but those so inclined may face serious complications in their intimate relationships. Fortunately, most partners attuned to the 3 understand the importance of moderation and self-control, and they can apply the brakes when necessary.

4

MOTIVATION: Stable, but generally passive. Natives of the 4 Sexual Consensus are strong-willed but usually don't take the initiative in love or sex. They dislike being labeled as passive or aggressive, as they embrace equality and mutual interaction in their relationships. Yet, they are more likely to follow a partner's lead than to accept the dominant role themselves.

RESPONSE: Average to good. These individuals are stable sensible, and dependable partners, averse to erotic escapades and cheap thrills. Males are reliable, loyal, and generous in their affections but tend to be somewhat conventional in lovemaking. Females are more sensitive, exhibiting endurance and steady intensity in bed. Both genders enjoy intimate contact. They avoid extreme emotions during sex and can appreciate a purely physical relationship without forming deep emotional bonds.

INHIBITIONS: Numerous inhibitions are associated with the 4 vibration, but no major hang-ups. Some who resonate with this vibration may be reluctant to experiment with new postures and techniques, and a minority are repulsed by oral sex. In rare cases, these aversions could lead to monotonous sex habits and a generally unsatisfying love life.

COMPATIBLE PARTNERS: Down-to-earth lovers who view sexuality as an earthy pleasure and do not insist on a romantic ingredient in their physical relationships are well suited to this temperament. Weak, sentimental, or idealistic partners are not compatible and the ensuing relationship would be mutually disappointing. Partners who rush through the sex act do not harmonize well with these deliberate individuals, who are masters of foreplay. They express steady intensity and prolong the sex act to enhance their own pleasure and bring their lovers greater enjoyment.

POSSIBLE SHORTCOMINGS: For the most part, natives of the 4 Sexual Consensus are well-adjusted and comfortable with their sexuality. A few can be closed-minded, prone to routine lovemaking, and unwilling to experiment with new or more stimulating techniques. Impulsive and highly responsive lovers may cause these individuals to pull away and regard sex as an unwelcome obligatory chore. Overall sexual performance, or the lack of it, largely depends on the attitudes and actions of their partners, and those who take the time to coax these individuals into a more responsive frame of mind will be rewarded by their steady intensity and attentiveness.

5

MOTIVATION: Assertive. These natives make no secret of the fact that they enjoy sex. Dynamic, energetic, and direct, they enthusiastically take the initiative. Rather than waiting for a desired partner to make a move, they will pursue a desired mate, demonstrating great persistence. They're forthright, say what they mean, and mean what they say. If they allow a lover to dominate, it's merely a tactic they use to help them achieve what they want.

RESPONSE: Natives of the 5 Sexual Consensus are intense, passionate, open-minded, and deeply sensuous. Their natural curiosity and willingness to experiment with unconventional lovemaking techniques contribute to their allure as fun-loving, stimulating partners. The men are charismatic and sociable, deeply engrossed in physical sensations. The women are stylish, glamorous, captivating lovers, typically stable and well-balanced but prone to impulsiveness with the right partner. Both genders place a strong emphasis on a mate's physical appearance, and less attractive suitors won't get far with these picky individuals. They don't demand emotional attachment in sex and often prefer to establish physical relationships purely for erotic gratification.

INHIBITIONS: Usually, no serious sexual hang-ups are associated with this vibration, although emotional instability may exist in some individuals.

COMPATIBLE PARTNERS: Imaginative, assertive lovers with a curious nature, a flair for adventure, and a strong sex drive interact well with natives of the 5 Sexual Consensus. Because good looks is a prerequisite, attractive mates will find themselves more readily accepted. Weak, inhibited people, and those who approach sex routinely, are incompatible with this vibration and may find themselves overwhelmed by this ardent lover. Deeply sentimental and co-dependent partners are also ill-suited to this temperament.

POSSIBLE SHORTCOMINGS: Natural sensuality is one of the most appealing attributes of those who share the 5 Sexual Consensus; yet the same quality can work to their detriment. Some of these individuals feel prey to excessive indulgence. They cling to physical sensation and recklessly pursue orgasmic gratification, sacrificing too much for temporary release. Many confuse love with sex, mistaking one for the other. This habit must be overcome, sooner than later, or their love affairs may be beset by constant chaos.

6

MOTIVATION: Natives of the 6 Sexual Consensus might appear passive, but they are quite resourceful and determined. They may assume a more dominant role when they feel insecure, which happens often. They are very adept at using emotional tactics to sway an uncompromising mate and usually get what they want.

RESPONSE: Varies. These individuals are often prone to unpredictable behavior in physical relationships. They can be passionate, sensitive, and creative, willing to try new and unconventional lovemaking techniques as they eagerly strive to please. But in the next breath, they can be flirtatious, sarcastic, and tactless. Their response during intimate encounters largely depends on their current partner's approach to sexuality. They typically exude the admirable traits of the 6 vibration when love and affection are present in their relationships.

INHIBITIONS: Numerous, but a patient lover can assist these 6-natives in overcoming virtually all of their sexual and emotional inhibitions. Common issues associated with this vibration are lack of confidence and discomfort with nudity, especially among females. These challenges can bring tension and a sense of restriction or prudishness into their love lives, potentially leading to deep feelings of guilt and frustration.

COMPATIBLE PARTNERS: Men who resonate with the 6 Sexual Consensus interact well with lovers who share a similar temperament. They don't appreciate criticism or attempts to dominate them, thus making aggressive partners unsuitable. Imaginative yet stable partners are the most likely candidates to bring out their better qualities. Women attuned to this vibration are very responsive to passionate, expressive lovers who take the initiative and strive to unlock new dimensions of pleasure without going to extremes or becoming abusive. Those who seek erotic gratification without romantic involvement are incompatible.

POSSIBLE SHORTCOMINGS: For these individuals, the natural depth and sensitivity instilled by the 6 vibration can be significant assets but may also work to their detriment. Thus, moodiness, depression, and melancholy are the main pitfalls here, especially if a romantic breakup is imminent. Some of the women may take revenge on an unfaithful lover by responding with illicit flings of their own. When a relationship goes off the rails in this way, they may become bitter, aloof partners.

7

MOTIVATION: Those attuned to the 7 Sexual Consensus may approach sex with high hopes but sometimes unrealistic expectations. Typically, they assume a passive role, which doesn't mean that they are weak or submissive, but rather, they prefer to let their partner take the lead. They don't usually pursue prospective mates that spark their interest; instead, they let it be known that they're available and interested, and then wait for the other person to make the first move.

RESPONSE: Variable. These individuals typically don't display fiery aggression or enthusiasm for physical intimacy found with some other vibrations. On the contrary, they might seem cool and detached, even during the act of sex itself. They don't usually reach great heights of ecstasy, and when they do experience pleasure, they might hide their true feelings. But if a sexual relationship becomes romantically significant, they are apt to be more passionate and responsive. Though slow to warm, they exhibit remarkable depth and sensuality once they grow comfortable with a perceptive mate.

INHIBITIONS: Numerous, and sometimes many. Those attuned to the 7 vibration may seem sexually progressive, but many of these individuals are deeply insecure and lack self-confidence, which can sometimes lead to a repressed sex drive. Both men and women are usually balanced although sometimes overly analytical, which might cause some partners to perceive them as hyper-critical. Feelings of guilt or shame are often drivers of inhibitions in 7-natives.

COMPATIBLE PARTNERS: Passionate, aggressive mates are not compatible with this temperament. Narrow-minded and overly critical partners are unsuitable as well. Ideally, an understanding, sensitive lover with a respect for moderation, but who takes the initiative in bed, is the ideal match for natives of the 7 vibration. Extremists, egotists, and those with addictive personalities must be avoided.

POSSIBLE SHORTCOMINGS: Repressed sexuality and a lack of enthusiasm for physical intimacy are the main pitfalls of the 7 Sexual Consensus. Unrealistic expectations in pursuing the "perfect" love can also be problematic. In rare instances, a complete lack of interest or outright aversion to sexual relations may develop, leading to an overly critical or disinterested attitude toward sex and romance in general.

8

MOTIVATION: Assertive, but in a practical sense. Natives of the 8 Sexual Consensus are assertive, stable, and dependable, but sometimes a bit old-fashioned and set in their ways. They know what they want in a relationship and pursue it without hesitation. They are the drivers in their romances and are usually dominant in sex. However, if asked, they will allow their partner to lead.

RESPONSE: Very good. These individuals are affectionate, not embarrassed to show their feelings in private and in public, and they're stubbornly determined in physical relationships. The men are strong-willed, fit, energetic, and eager to satisfy, although some may be self-absorbed and come across as selfish or inconsiderate. The women attuned to this vibration are more affectionate and adaptable than the men but still deliberate in physical intimacy. They enjoy extended lovemaking and exhibit a steady, earthy intensity in bed. Both genders are open-minded and curious. Unconventional relationships and offbeat or exotic sex practices appeal to them, but they never force their partners beyond their comfort zone.

INHIBITIONS: No significant inhibitions are associated with the 8 Sexual Consensus. Minor hang-ups may develop if emotions come into play, especially when these individuals are matched with incompatible partners and arguments flare, which may spark feelings of self-consciousness or guilt. Overall, however, these individuals are well-adjusted and quite capable of enjoying a healthy and active sex life.

COMPATIBLE PARTNERS: The 8 vibration harmonizes well with most vibrations, including other 8-natives. Partners who view sex as a natural, earthy pleasure and can enjoy physical intimacy without emotional entanglements are ideally compatible. Resourceful, self-reliant partners are also a good match. Involvements with emotional weaklings and impulsive romantics should be avoided.

POSSIBLE SHORTCOMINGS: The primary pitfall of the 8 Sexual Consensus is that individuals may seek orgasmic release so fervently that they come across as selfish and deprive their partners of satisfaction. This tendency must be checked early in the relationship, or neither party will derive much enjoyment from intimacy. Men attuned to this vibration may come across as overbearing or demanding, causing more sensitive partners to pull back and seek intimacy elsewhere.

9

MOTIVATION: Passive. These individuals usually avoid taking on a dominant role and prefer to be pursued rather than to pursue others. In sexual relations, they are cooperative, responsive, and open to trying novel techniques and positions, as long as their partners take the lead. Some of these individuals are shy or self-conscious and will enjoy greater compatibility with a supportive, understanding partner.

RESPONSE: Good. Those who resonate with the 9 Sexual Consensus may seem aloof or disinterested, but they can be very responsive under the right circumstances. They are sensitive, empathetic partners with an open-minded approach to sex. Men are imaginative and resourceful, though some might be perceived as repressed or clinical in their approach to sex. Women are tolerant, gentle, thoughtful companions motivated by a strong desire for security and an urge to please.

INHIBITIONS: Despite their apparent open-mindedness, 9-natives can be reserved, cautious, even suspicious, and prone to hold back their feelings for reasons likely rooted in painful past relationships. They fear rejection and loneliness, and they don't like being perceived as vulnerable.

COMPATIBLE PARTNERS: Unstable partners prone to flighty, impulsive, or promiscuous behavior are not compatible with natives of the 9 Sexual Consensus, who want stability and permanence. They expect their lovers to be strong, supportive, and reliable. Their ideal match will be found among potential lovers who seek a meaningful involvement embracing both love and sex. Because many of these individuals constantly fret about their love affairs failing unexpectedly, they need partners who will create a calm and reassuring environment in which they can feel loved and secure.

POSSIBLE SHORTCOMINGS: The principal pitfall of the 9 Sexual Consensus is that its natives may become disillusioned and bitter or manipulative. They may sour on love and adopt a fatalistic attitude toward romance and other areas of life. Some 9-natives who have suffered heartbreak in the past may repress their emotions to the point that they never allow themselves to experience happiness or fulfillment in love and sex.

11

MOTIVATION: Individuals who resonate with the 11 Sexual Consensus are friendly, outgoing, perceptive, and quick to recognize opportunities for forging new relationships. They are prone to secrecy, can be subtly manipulative, and at times exhibit passive-aggressive behavior. They desire stimulating and unconventional sexual expression, so they often assume the lead, shaping their love affairs, and lovers, to their liking. However, if deep emotions come into play, some of these individuals may lose confidence and assume a more passive role, allowing their partner to take the initiative.

RESPONSE: Highly favorable. In physical relationships, both men and women are intense, adaptable, sensual, and imaginative. Their approach to intimacy is innovative and progressive. They don't require love in a sexual partnership, but its presence inspires them toward deeper displays of affection. Fantasies play a significant role in their erotic interactions. Some 11-males may become unstable when emotions are too involved, while women are open-minded, curious, energetic, and imbued with significant sex appeal and a vivid imagination.

INHIBITIONS: Some 11-natives have a strong aversion to nudity. The women are relatively uninhibited, although a few may prefer to keep lovemaking in darkness. The men can be surprisingly shy or self-conscious, and some worry obsessively about the consequences of their sexual escapades, although they are unlikely to change their behavior and rein in their appetite for sexual adventure.

COMPATIBLE PARTNERS: Sensuous, assertive, and fun-loving partners are compatible with this temperament. Egotists, extremists, and those with a clinical or overly practical approach to sex don't align well with 11-natives. Physical appeal is an important prerequisite in their sexual relationships, particularly among men, who often find unique or striking beauty in their companions irresistible. However, relationships built primarily on physical attraction rarely work well for them.

POSSIBLE SHORTCOMINGS: Naivety and indiscretion are the major pitfalls of the 11 Sexual Consensus. Some of these individuals are secretive and not particularly faithful. They are constantly on the go, seeking out attractive and unconventional people, and they find it difficult to say "no" to temptation. This shortcoming often gets them into trouble. They place too much trust in short-term partners they barely know, and as a result, they can be easily manipulated or deceived in sexual relations. Cultivating better judgment, being more selective in choosing their sex partners, and learning self-control will go a long way to help these individuals find happiness and fulfillment in their intimate relationships.

14

MOTIVATION: Dominant; assertive. Individuals attuned to the 14 Sexual Consensus are among the most sensual and have the greatest appetites for physical pleasure in the number spectrum. They do not procrastinate when someone sparks their interest, and they come straight to the point. Once aroused, they swiftly assume the dominant role. They rely on their physical magnetism and charisma to achieve their desires, and almost always obtain what they want.

RESPONSE: Exceptional. These men and women lavish affection on their partners to the point of extravagance, and they're willing to take risks without much concern about the consequences. They do not insist on forming deep emotional connections in bed and can enjoy a purely physical relationship for the erotic pleasure it offers. They are daring, original, and frank in their approach to lovemaking. Women are fascinating, dramatic, often glamorous, and inclined to experiment with innovative or unconventional sexual practices and techniques. They can achieve orgasmic release frequently and with ease. Men can be somewhat selfish and over-eager during intimacy, which may occasionally detract from mutual satisfaction.

INHIBITIONS: A few individuals under the 14 Sexual Consensus exhibit peculiar fears or phobias in sexual interactions.

One such proclivity is a compulsive fear of contracting sexually transmitted diseases or other ailments from their partners. However, most do not have significant inhibitions, as long as their emotions aren't too involved. When a physical relationship becomes romantic, they may become withdrawn and painfully self-conscious.

COMPATIBLE PARTNERS: Nearly every vibration in the number spectrum harmonizes with the 14. People who tend to be old-fashioned, those with strong moral convictions, and those who take a routine or overly practical approach to sex and love are least likely to find fulfillment with these individuals. Intense partners with a strong sex drive and who can appreciate the pleasure of physical intimacy are compatible, although they may be less so if emotional attachments form.

POSSIBLE SHORTCOMINGS: Many 14-natives mistake sexual attraction for love, which can lead to tumultuous love affairs and broken relationships. They are willing to risk all for a good time or a sexual conquest but often come up short. A few are predisposed to addictive behaviors and continually seek out physical stimulation, sometimes selfishly rushing through sex acts in search of immediate gratification, yet realizing little or no reward.

16

MOTIVATION: Individuals attuned to the 16 Sexual Consensus reject the labels of "passive" and "aggressive," and they dislike stereotypes. They believe that cooperative interaction is the key to mutual fulfillment, and any two partners can attain happiness if they invest the effort. As long as emotions aren't too involved, they enjoy open, reciprocal relationships, often assuming the dominant role but sometimes encouraging their partner to take the lead to spice things up.

RESPONSE: Exceptional. These individuals are passionate and responsive sexual partners. Their relationships typically run deep and sometimes take an unconventional or provocative turn. They don't demand love, but they become much more passionate and responsive when an emotional bond exists with a partner. They frequently employ sex as a medium to express their feelings and affection.

INHIBITIONS: Varies, based on personality. Emotional types grapple with guilt around sex and may have an aversion to nudity. Practical types typically don't have inhibitions and take a logical approach to sexuality. Some 16-females attempt to hide their true feelings fearing that they might lose control or a partner might take advantage of them.

COMPATIBLE PARTNERS: Partners who embrace an earthy, conventional approach to lovemaking, and those who exhibit aggressive behavior, are not good matches for this temperament. Progressive, empathetic, and sensitive lovers are highly compatible. Although many 16-natives have minor inhibitions and insecurities, lovers who are similarly inhibited or insecure make good mates as their interaction will be built on a foundation of mutual understanding.

POSSIBLE SHORTCOMINGS: The main pitfalls of the 16 Sexual Consensus are poor judgment, indiscretion, occasional dishonesty to cover their indiscretions, and a tendency to choose unsuitable lovers based on looks or a good pickup line. Natives of the 16 need to be far more selective in their choice of partners. Impulsiveness is a potentially significant pitfall and may sometimes unleash chaos in love affairs.

19

MOTIVATION: Dominant; assertive. Those who resonate with the 19 Sexual Consensus are open-minded and direct in physical intimacy but also tolerant and patient. They tend to vacillate between desiring change and wanting to try new things, on the one hand, and clinging to the familiarity of old-fashioned or conservative views, on the other. This seeming contradiction is, again, due to the competing influence of the 1 and 9 comprising this master vibration. Despite this, 19-natives are highly intelligent, rather calculating at times, and they know what they want in a relationship, although they don't necessarily know how to achieve it. Most of these individuals are charismatic, often the dominant partner, and quick to take the lead.

RESPONSE: These men and women respond favorably to unconventional ideas and colorful, eccentric lovers. They're receptive to new and unusual lovemaking techniques as well as non-traditional relationships. They instinctively sense a lover's desires and work diligently to enhance mutual pleasure. Vivid erotic fantasies may underlie some of their interactions. Men are more down-to-earth in their approach to sex, while women are sensual, dramatic, and playful, sometimes prone to teasing, and more inclined to experiment with exotic positions.

INHIBITIONS: Few or none, though some 19-natives may exhibit brief episodes of inferiority or be unwilling to openly show physical pleasure or emotions. This reticence is usually rooted in painful childhood memories. A patient lover can help them work through and overcome these psychological feelings.

COMPATIBLE PARTNERS: Fun-loving, open-minded, naturally inquisitive mates who are willing to try anything once in their approach to sex are compatible with these individuals. Confident, progressive partners, and those with an eclectic worldview, are also a good match. Lovers who are too practical or rigidly adhere to conventional norms will struggle to connect with 19-natives. Flighty or self-centered partners, and those who become highly emotional during sex, should be avoided. The 19 vibration combines a unique blend of independence and emotional depth, requiring a partner who can appreciate and interact well with these traits.

POSSIBLE SHORTCOMINGS: A common characteristic of the 19 Sexual Consensus is straining for sexual release but failing to achieve it. Some 19-natives may resort to selfishness or fail to consider their mate's feelings out of frustration. Fortunately, only a small minority are affected by this pitfall, and they typically take a pessimistic or apathetic approach to love and sex that will discourage potential suitors' interest. Rarely, men who resonate with the 19 may express a quick temper and anger control issues, while women may engage in unhealthy or risky sexual practices. However, the majority of these individuals are stable and have good judgment along with a sense of moderation that will enable them to build satisfying and enduring relationships.

22

MOTIVATION: Aggressive yet sensible, adaptable, and down-to-earth. Individuals attuned to the 22 Sexual Consensus are resourceful and strong-willed. In physical intimacy, they are honest and direct, though sometimes blunt. They often take the dominant role but rarely exhibit controlling behavior. While relatively open-minded, they're not particularly interested in exotic lovemaking techniques and have little patience for flighty, irresponsible partners. If their mates lack initiative, they will move to spice things up. They seek a mutually satisfying relationship built on trust and mutual respect, and they are considerate of their partners' needs and desires.

RESPONSE: Very good. While these individuals typically don't radiate sensuality, they are often praised for their warmth and earnestness. Some are capable of considerable passion when coaxed by a partner who understands their nuances. They thrive with stable but sensitive mates who can bring out their best qualities in bed. Men attuned to the 22 Sexual Consensus approach sex as an earthy, mundane pleasure and don't require deep emotional involvement in their physical connections. Women can be quite vivacious, affectionate, and imaginative under the right circumstances.

INHIBITIONS: Generally, none. Most 22-natives are stable, confident, and sexually well-adjusted. A few may prefer to avoid some erotic practices, especially oral sex, or are averse to extended foreplay. However, these inhibitions can usually be overcome with the support of an empathetic lover.

COMPATIBLE PARTNERS: Potential companions who are inclined to vacillation, erratic behavior, or extremes, and those who are emotionally weak or overly dramatic, are not good matches. Likewise, those interested in offbeat erotic practices or non-conventional relationships are not compatible with this temperament. Sensible, down-to-earth lovers who appreciate the pleasures of a physical relationship without complicated entanglements harmonize best with 22-natives.

POSSIBLE SHORTCOMINGS: The potential pitfalls for the 22 Sexual Consensus are a tendency for routine lovemaking and, in some instances, repressed sexuality. Another challenge is that ultra-practical 22-natives may approach sexual intimacy so methodically that it discourages mutual satisfaction. When lovemaking becomes lackluster or monotonous, either or both partners may be tempted to move on to a more appealing relationship. The 22 vibration installs deep responsiveness and the ability to derive immense pleasure from physical intimacy, but these individuals need patient, insightful partners who will encourage them to unlock new levels of sexual freedom and expression.

Chapter 6
Determining Your Karmic Liability

Almost every adult has at some point experienced setbacks and disappointments in love and every other facet of life. Some of us adeptly handle these upsets, others struggle with them, while yet others throw up their hands in despair and accept defeat.

How an individual reacts to the ups and downs of daily life often depends on a variety of factors, including their level of optimism, determination, and self-awareness. Individuals who acknowledge their challenges and actively strive to circumvent or overcome them are less likely to suffer disappointment or failure in romance than those who lack these personal qualities and are at the mercy of their emotions.

Identifying the roots of love-related problems, however, isn't always straightforward. Some people go through life seeking but never achieving a meaningful love relationship. But what if we could accurately identify the character flaws and other obstacles that block our path to meaningful relationships? Then, our chances of attaining genuine happiness would surely be improved.

The next crucial aspect of numerology that we will explore in this chapter, which we refer to as "karmic liabilities" or "karmic lessons," enables us to gain insights into some of the roadblocks in our relationships and that we might otherwise encounter in our journey through life. A straightforward mathematical formula enables us to identify these land mines that may trigger discord in our relationships. Quite simply, for this procedure, we look for primary vibrations absent from a person's full name at birth. Any digit between 1 and 9 that does not appear somewhere in the name at least once is identified as a karmic lesson. Once these lessons have been pinpointed, we can choose to ignore the signposts reflected in our love chart or apply them and thereby avert the heartbreak that casts a dark shadow in the lives of so many people today.

In numerology, the nine karmic lessons and their corresponding numerical values are:

(1) individuality

(2) composure

(3) self-expression

(4) organization

(5) moderation

(6) responsibility

(7) stability

(8) generosity

(9) self-awareness.

Each lesson represents a potential roadblock that may trip you up, either once in a while or often, as you go through life. Until a karmic lesson is recognized and mastered, it will continue to exert a disruptive effect on your life.

Depending on your mood and the state of your day-to-day affairs, you might glance at the list above and imagine yourself deficient in some or many of these areas. Yet, as we've discussed before, self-assessing your own strengths and weaknesses with true objectivity is virtually impossible. For most of us, the only yardstick we currently possess consists of the moral and social values we were given as children—values handed down from previous generations, often based on impractical or outdated beliefs. This is where the science of numerology can prove its worth, providing a clear picture of the karmic liabilities or lessons that you must recognize and overcome.

Numerologists believe karmic lessons are determined at birth. At any time while you are growing up, you might recognize these pitfalls and choose to overcome them. Once a karmic lesson has been mastered, it ceases to play a significant role in your life. Thus, any lessons that you've already overcome should no longer affect your romances and other pursuits. However, if you've neglected to confront a karmic lesson, it will continue to surface in your life, challenging you, until you master it and cleanse its effects from your daily life.

As an interesting footnote, based on my analysis of more than 5,000 love charts I've compiled over the years, the number "7" is the most common karmic lesson, and it is missing in about 50 percent of all charts. The numbers 2, 4, 6, and 8 are also missing in many numerology charts. Karmic lessons observed less frequently are 1, 3, and 5, while 9 only rarely appears as a karmic lesson.

A few more interesting insights: approximately 35 percent of numerology charts reflect one karmic lesson; 45 percent indicate two karmic lessons, and 19 percent reflect three or more. A mere one percent have no karmic lessons, making this condition exceedingly rare.

To gain a deeper understanding of your own Karmic Liability, or the karmic lessons challenging your mate or potential partner, refer to the interpretations provided below.

1

Indecision and lack of confidence are hallmarks of the 1 karmic lesson. Individuals with this karmic liability often fail to take the initiative, attempt to take shortcuts in romance, and either postpone plans or execute them prematurely. They allow others to control their lives, which dampens or ruins their romantic prospects. Because they lack the courage to express their feelings openly and confidently, potential partners may perceive them as uninteresting, detached, or weak. It is difficult for them to achieve happiness in love or success in life when they anticipate that their relationships will fail before they start.

To master this karmic liability and enhance your romantic prospects, you must learn to stand tall and be the initiator. Be confident, proud, and courageous. Cultivate self-awareness and mindfulness to help you better understand your emotions and actions, which in turn will strengthen your confidence in your own decisions. Step out of your shadow, don't be afraid to express yourself. Let your vibrant personality shine, and you'll experience an immediate improvement in your love life.

2

The 2 karmic lesson usually suggests a tendency to appear timid or ambivalent in romantic pursuits. Individuals with this lesson are prone to procrastinate and put off decisions in all aspects of their life, especially romance. They resign themselves to hoping that things will work out and often depend on chance to decide the outcomes. This can lead to countless missed opportunities and give prospective lovers who appeal to you the impression that you are not interested in them.

To master this karmic liability, you must accept that love isn't accidental—it requires proactive steps to attract a suitable partner and build a mutually satisfying relationship. Cultivate willpower and determination, let your natural depth and sensitivity shine, and don't be afraid to reach for what you want. Even if you lack assertiveness, your many other redeeming qualities may appeal to a wide range of potential mates. Learn to trust your judgment. Invest your time and energy wisely, pursue goals with confidence and determination, and above all, remember: you deserve happiness. As you learn to be more determined and gain clarity, you'll be able to make crucial decisions more easily, leading to better outcomes in romance and every other aspect of your life.

3

The 3 karmic lesson indicates a failure to communicate effectively or an inability to express your thoughts and feelings. Some individuals with this karmic lesson may speak a lot, but their words lack substance. When boldness is needed, they hesitate, and when creative solutions are required to move forward, they fall into a rut. Their goals in love and life cannot be achieved until they develop the skill of self-expression and let their creativity flow freely into their thoughts and actions.

Mastering this karmic liability will take time and effort, but it need not be a painful ordeal. Developing eloquent verbal and written communication skills can be an interesting learning adventure with immediate rewards. Take the first step on this journey by embracing a determination to speak what's on your mind, say what you mean, and mean what you say. Be more dramatic, outspoken, and imaginative. At the same time, strive to understand, not just to be understood. Communication is a two-way street that involves both expressing your feelings clearly and understanding the feelings of others. When you encounter obstacles or disappointments in your quest to master this lesson, don't let discouragement cloud your enthusiasm. Open and honest communication with a flair will significantly improve your romantic life and overall prospects in life.

4

The 4 karmic lesson is associated with disorganization, impracticality, rigid thinking, or a combination of these pitfalls. It can also indicate that a person is stuck in a quagmire of narrow-minded thinking or inflexibility, which can only be remedied by opening up one's mind, embracing new ideas, and making a concerted effort to be more tolerant. If you have this karmic liability, you may exhibit general disorganization in your emotional affairs and broader life. This contributes to confusion and dissatisfaction in your affairs and undermines your happiness. You may be habitually late for appointments and social engagements, or you might not show up at all. Sentimental dates on your calendar may be overlooked, leaving partners wondering whether you're preoccupied or don't care about them.

To master this lesson, you need to organize your life—your belongings, daily activities, goals, finances, and emotional landscape. Cultivate attention to detail and a clear focus on what matters the most to you in your life. Avoid cycles of confused activities and wasted efforts. Approach romance and daily life with a sense of calm and clarity. Avoid procrastination. Establish a clear plan of action for achieving what you want, and pursue those goals with utmost efficiency. Use tools such as planners and apps to organize your time and responsibilities efficiently. If you are burdened with narrow-mindedness or judgmental thinking, embrace a fresh, open-minded outlook and strive to see the best in others rather than the worst. Mastering this karmic lesson is achievable and doesn't have to be difficult. Once accomplished, all aspects of your daily life will begin to flow smoothly and harmoniously.

5

The 5 karmic lesson serves as a warning against over-indulgence. Those who have this karmic liability are drawn to physical stimulation and may take unnecessary risks, especially for erotic pleasure. This thrill-seeking behavior could lead to addictive tendencies and negative consequences. In romance, these individuals prioritize sex over love or confuse the two, causing harm to their partners, inadvertently or intentionally.

If you have this karmic liability, you need to develop willpower and self-control, refrain from risky behaviors, and deepen your understanding of love as a form of emotional intimacy rather than merely a physical connection. Seek healthy outlets for your energy, such as sports or hobbies, to satisfy your desire for stimulation in positive ways. Develop a balanced approach to relationships and daily life in general. Learn to distinguish between emotional intimacy and sexual attraction, and build meaningful relationships that don't rely solely on sex. The sooner you learn this lesson, the faster you'll be able to cultivate a happy and satisfying love life.

6

The 6 vibration pertains to domestic responsibility, family, marriage, and home life. If you have this karmic lesson, it implies that you have avoided these life experiences or failed to embrace their significance. You might have shied away from intimacy and commitment, fearing that close relationships will end in disappointment. Some individuals with this karmic liability establish committed relationships but pursue illicit affairs on the side, believing their current partner will abandon them, and if they have another partner to fall back on, they won't have to endure loneliness. This is a self-defeating cycle that guarantees turbulent relationships and heartbreak.

To overcome this karmic liability, you need to embrace the emotional and spiritual value of an enduring relationship and establish one. Understand that avoiding intimacy, or resorting to infidelity, are pitfalls of this karmic lesson, and can only be mastered by immersing yourself in deep intimacy. A committed relationship need not be a terrifying or painful experience—it can be a source of fulfillment and joy. By learning to trust and be comfortable with one partner, you can experience the bliss of deep commitment and the beauty of a shared journey. In this way, you can master this karmic lesson and welcome profound happiness and fulfillment into your life.

7

The 7 vibration represents analysis, wisdom, justice, and spirituality. When the 7 karmic lesson appears, it indicates an absence of one or more of these attributes. Impulsivity, jumping to hasty conclusions, cynicism, and intolerance may manifest with this karmic liability. Individuals grappling with this lesson are prone to impulsiveness in love and sex, although they may exhibit good judgment in other aspects of their daily lives. They fear loneliness and rejection, which can cause them to overreact to minor conflicts, provoking suspicions, often unfounded, of a partner's actions and doubts about their affection or loyalty. Arguments, accusations, and irrational thinking may quickly escalate into emotional turmoil and failed relationships.

Mastering the 7 karmic lesson will require cultivating good judgment, balance, and emotional self-control. Before reacting to unfounded suspicions and letting your imagination run wild, stop and think things through. Strive to be calm and reasonable, maintaining honest communication with your mate at all times. When you hit rough spots, as will invariably happen even in the most stable relationship, avoid jumping to conclusions, and don't surrender to impulsive behavior. Aim for a rational and constructive response. Take advantage of the analytical power, keen insight, and deep wisdom inherent in the 7 vibration when its positive attributes are expressed. Cultivating calm, rational thinking and honing your approach to relationships will help you avoid heartache and forge a stable, enduring romance and a lifetime of happiness.

8

The 8 vibration pertains to material success, wealth, ego, and leadership. As a karmic lesson, the 8 is dual-faceted, warning of extravagance, poor financial judgment, and faulty judgment on the one hand, and the potential for egotism, selfishness, and a domineering personality on the other. Both shortcomings can create chaos in romantic relationships, with financial mismanagement provoking stress and tension, and ego-driven behaviors causing conflict and dissatisfaction. In extreme instances, individuals grappling with this karmic lesson might be perceived as tyrannical, cruel, or abusive.

For those confronting financial challenges, mastering the 8 karmic lesson requires cultivating better money management skills and controlling impulsive or extravagant spending. This could mean developing a budget, staying on top of bills and other financial obligations, and keeping unrestrained spending in check. Those struggling with egotism or control issues should cultivate humility, flexibility, tolerance, and a willingness to compromise. This might involve practicing active listening, making a conscious effort to recognize the needs and desires of others, and learning to share or yield control in relationships. Mastering the 8 karmic liability, in either form, will help you create healthier and more balanced romantic connections, and it will bring positivity to other facets of your daily life.

9

The 9 vibration, when positively expressed, represents maturity, knowledge, acceptance, kindness, willing sacrifice, and universal consciousness. As a karmic lesson, it indicates an absence of one or more of these attributes. It is rarely found in numerology charts. Those who have this karmic liability may be perceived as cynical, bitter, aloof, or lacking emotional warmth. Some are hypercritical, intolerant, or selfish, which can kindle feelings of loneliness, isolation, and a pessimistic life outlook. There may be a failure to recognize or appreciate the profound joy that can be derived from human warmth and meaningful interaction.

Mastering this karmic lesson involves opening up to human experience and overcoming the dark clouds that might loom on your emotional and spiritual horizon. You'll need to recalibrate your interest in the human experience and the world around you, becoming more involved in the plight of others. Challenge yourself to be more caring, tolerant, and optimistic. You may need to refine your social skills and step out of your comfort zone, opening your heart to human interactions that you've avoided in the past. Taking the first steps might be uncomfortable, but the rewards you'll reap from overcoming this karmic lesson are immense. Unlock your heart, let yourself feel, or fall in love, and you'll open the door to a brighter, more meaningful, and rewarding life.

Chapter 7
Guide to the Transcendent Challenge

*A*nother facet of numerology that can significantly impact romance and other aspects of daily life is the Transcendent Challenge. Based on a simple process of arithmetic, it permits further self-analysis and reveals the most favorable character traits that an individual could develop (attributes), as well as their negative traits or shortcomings (pitfalls). These insights, properly applied, can profoundly influence our love relationships and broader day-to-day affairs. Most people lack the objectivity to accurately identify their strengths and shortcomings, in part because these qualities may be hidden or not routinely expressed. However, numerology can bring these insights to light and suggest a constructive path to realize positive change in ourselves.

The interpretive guidelines presented in these next pages reveal the attributes and pitfalls associated with each of the nine Transcendent Challenge vibrations. Look up the passage corresponding to your Transcendent Challenge, or that of your mate or a potential partner, to gain clarity on its significance in your life.

1

ATTRIBUTES: Innovative, self-reliant, inquisitive, inventive, persistent, ambitious, original thinker, leadership skills, motivated, confident, charitable, problem solver, courageous.

PITFALLS:

A tendency toward stubbornness, which may manifest as an unwillingness to accept others' ideas or advice due to your self-reliance and confidence.

Impulsiveness may surface due to your innovative and daring spirit, potentially leading to hasty or reckless decisions.

A dominating nature might develop when your leadership skills become controlling behavior.

Insensitivity is a possible risk when your persistent and problem-solving mindset overshadows the emotional needs of others.

Impatience may be exacerbated by your desire for progress and results, leading to restlessness and intolerance of delays.

Arrogance can surface when your confidence grows into a superiority complex.

An uncompromising attitude may arise when your original thinking leads to an inflexible approach.

An overbearing tendency can develop when your self-reliance and confidence manifest as disregard for others' feelings or abilities.

Being overly competitive can occur when your need for accomplishment overshadows cooperative efforts.

A propensity to burnout is a possibility if your persistence and motivation lead to overworking and exhaustion.

Isolation may develop when your self-reliance leads to a lack of social connection or feelings of loneliness.

Perfectionism might become a burden when your high-achiever personality and desire for excellence lead to unrealistic expectations of yourself and others, causing stress and disappointment.

Resistance to criticism can be a potential issue when your strong confidence and belief in your ideas make you resistant to feedback, potentially impeding your growth and progress.

Workaholic tendencies can become a risk factor when your high level of motivation and persistence causes work to be overemphasized at the expense of your personal relationships.

YOUR CHALLENGE:

Based on the foregoing characteristics, your challenge is to balance your strong sense of self and pioneering spirit with the ability to listen, accept other viewpoints, and collaborate. Your innovative and highly motivated nature can be a powerful force but may sometimes spark impatience, inflexibility, or an overly competitive spirit. In the context of romantic relationships, these traits can cause a partner to feel overshadowed or unappreciated. Remember that successful relationships require understanding, reciprocation, and mutual respect. Value your partner's perspectives and feelings as much as your own.

Your strength lies not just in your ability to lead, but also in your capacity to inspire, motivate, and love deeply. Take the time to acknowledge others' input, express your affection and appreciation often, and strive to make your partner feel valued and cherished. Be careful to avoid burnout by setting unrealistic expectations, both professionally and personally, and know when to take a break.

Embrace the power of compromise. Remember that the journey can sometimes be just as important as the destination. Don't resist criticism, but see it as a chance for growth. The balancing act of dividing your energy between work and love may seem challenging, but achieving this equilibrium will significantly improve your overall satisfaction and the health of your romantic relationships.

2

ATTRIBUTES: Empathetic, tactful, compassionate, friendly, diplomatic, cooperative, good listener, calming presence, fair-minded, optimistic, loyal, easy-going, supportive, patient, forgiving, intuitive.

PITFALLS:

Hypersensitivity can be an issue when your empathetic and compassionate nature makes you susceptible to emotional upheaval.

Indecisiveness can stem from your diplomatic nature and your desire for conflict avoidance.

A tendency to be submissive is a potential pitfall when your caring and trusting disposition allows others to take advantage of you.

Self-sacrifice can occur when your desire for harmony causes you to sidestep confrontations or difficult conversations.

Dependence on others for validation or approval can stem from your need to be helpful and appreciated.

Feelings of resentment, which may brew if your efforts to help and support are not reciprocated or acknowledged.

Lack of assertiveness might develop when your calming presence and patient disposition hinder your ability to express your personal needs or define boundaries.

A tendency to self-neglect, which can manifest when your compassion for others causes you to overlook your own well-being.

Passive-aggressive behavior can occur when your desire for peaceful resolutions causes you to express negative feelings indirectly.

Emotional volatility can be a pitfall because your highly sensitive nature can provoke exaggerated emotional responses.

Victim mentality or martyrdom may arise when you are forced into a position of having to be overly accommodating, which can cause you to feel exploited or wronged.

YOUR CHALLENGE:

With the 2 Transcendent Challenge, you must establish a balance between your natural tendency to care for others and the need to care for yourself. Your empathetic and supportive nature makes you an exceptional friend, partner, and confidant, but it can also lead you to neglect or forfeit your own needs. In the realm of romance, it's crucial to remember that it's not only healthy to prioritize your needs and feelings—it's a necessary part of building a healthy, balanced relationship. Develop the courage to assert your own needs and insist upon boundaries, and resist the temptation to seek validation exclusively through your relationships. Strive to maintain your unique identity even as you navigate the complexities of intimacy. Avoid falling into patterns of passive-aggressive communication or exhibiting a victim mentality when things don't go as planned. Recognize that conflict and disagreements are a natural part of any relationship, and approach them as opportunities for growth and deeper understanding rather than sources of discord to be avoided. Through this balance, you will cultivate relationships that are both nurturing and mutually fulfilling.

3

ATTRIBUTES: Creative, artistic, original, emotionally deep, imaginative, observant, good communicator, optimistic, motivated, perceptive, fun-loving, inspired, culturally aware, gregarious, open to new ideas and experiences.

PITFALLS:

Inconsistency can be a problem when your many diverse interests hinder your ability to maintain focus.

Superficiality can arise if you dwell too much on external appearances and neglect deeper emotional and spiritual values.

Vanity can be a problem when your need for appreciation and admiration is exaggerated by excessive self-focus.

Neglect of details can inject mistakes and oversights into your affairs because you tend to focus on the big picture and might overlook some of its important parts.

Extravagance can be detrimental to your financial stability when you indulge in lavish or impulsive spending driven by your zest for the finer things in life.

Reluctance to commit may lead to missed relationship opportunities, which you'll likely blame on your wide-ranging interests, hectic life, and desire for freedom.

A tendency to exaggerate can lead you to inflate facts or experiences.

Sensitivity to criticism may spark temperamental moods, fueled by your desire for respect and need for validation.

Indecisiveness can undermine your progress and delay your goals because you have so many interests, and it's difficult to choose a particular path or focus.

Over-optimism can lead you to underestimate possible challenges in your relationships and in your broader life, which can lead to mistakes and setbacks.

Mood swings can occur when your emotional sensitivity and depth exert a destabilizing influence on your emotions.

YOUR CHALLENGE:

With the 3 Transcendent Challenge, you will benefit by learning to harness and focus your creativity and keen intellect on one goal at a time so you don't drown in a whirlpool of competing interests. You have artistic leanings you are capable of deep emotions, making you a desirable partner. However, these qualities can also spark erratic mood swings and an aversion to commitment. In romantic relationships, strive to be present, authentic, and emotionally consistent. Avoid the trap of focusing too much on external validation or approval, and instead nurture your self-confidence from within. Learn to appreciate the beauty of depth and detail, even as you revel in the bigger picture. Temper your optimism with a healthy dose of realism so you are ready to tackle obstacles in your path when they inevitably arise. By balancing your imaginative spirit with grounded, practical action, you can forge deep, emotionally rich, and fulfilling relationships.

4

ATTRIBUTES: Diligent, dependable, hard-working, efficient, detail-oriented, organized, disciplined, highly focused, patient, determined, stable, down-to-earth, honest, practical.

PITFALLS:

Stubbornness can result from being strongly committed to your views and established traditions, causing you to reject the opinions and ideas of others.

Being overly serious, which comes from your strong sense of duty and responsibility can make you seem stern or rigid, which in turn may result in lost opportunities for relaxation and fun in daily life.

Narrow-mindedness may color your life outlook, limiting your ability to accept new ideas and make changes in your life which may be necessary to improve existing conditions.

Pessimism may cloud your emotional landscape when your practical disposition hardens into a cynical life outlook.

Rigid thinking, or intolerance, can alienate people you care about when you become judgmental or overly opinionated.

Excessive caution may lead to stress, lost opportunities, and anxiety disorders, and can restrict your spontaneity.

Workaholic tendencies can wreak havoc on your personal life when you let your focus on work overshadow other aspects of your life, including leisure time and intimate relationships.

A lack of imagination, rooted in your detail-oriented mentality, can inhibit your ability to think creatively.

Monotony can impose a lack of variety or excitement in your life when you allow your preference for routine and predictability to cloud your emotional landscape.

Perfectionist tendencies may arise, causing you to become overly critical of yourself or to set unrealistic expectations.

YOUR CHALLENGE:

The 4 Transcendent Challenge encourages you to find a balance between a practical, detail-oriented approach to life and one that includes creativity and flexibility. In the realm of romance, know that relationships thrive on spontaneity, and variety keeps intimacy fresh and dynamic. Learn to let go of routine and predictability occasionally, so that you are open to new experiences and perspectives. Planting the seeds of joy and adventure in your spiritual garden is just as important as following the call of duty and responsibility. Learn to manage your criticism, both of yourself and others, to foster harmonious interaction with others. Embrace the possibility of change and the uncertainties it brings, viewing them as opportunities for growth rather than as threats to stability. Cultivate open emotions and be open to others' emotions, as this is key to building deeper, more satisfying relationships. By recognizing and working through these challenges, you can bring more balance, depth, and satisfaction into your love life.

5

ATTRIBUTES: Enthusiastic, free-spirited, spontaneous, fun-loving, bold, progressive, confident, adventurous, dramatic, inquisitive, energetic, willing to embrace new ideas, colorful friends, and unconventional lifestyles and philosophies with an open mind.

PITFALLS:

Impulsiveness can manifest when your love for adventure and change leads to hasty or ill-considered decisions.

Restlessness, stirred up by a free-spirited approach to life, could make it challenging for you to settle down or find peace in stillness.

Irresponsibility might be a problem when your desire for freedom causes you to neglect commitments and relationships.

Unpredictable behavior may erupt, prompted by your spontaneity and desire for change, even when it's not necessary or appropriate.

Aversion to deep intimacy and roots might make it difficult for you to commit to people, plans, or decisions.

A tendency to over-indulge may provoke concerns about being overweight and other health impacts; for some, it could open the door to potentially addictive behavior.

Tactlessness can spark resentment and hurt feelings when your spontaneous and direct nature prompts you to blurt out thoughtless or insensitive remarks.

Recklessness is a distinct possibility under the 5 Challenge, and you may be tempted to take unnecessary risks. This is usually not a good idea, and risk-taking should be avoided.

Discontentment, or an expectation that there should be more to your life, may leave you feeling perpetually unsatisfied.

YOUR CHALLENGE:

One aspect of the 5 Transcendent Challenge is learning to balance your appetite for freedom and lust for adventure with a grounded sense of responsibility. It is also crucial to avoid taking unnecessary risks that could lead to physical injury. A free-spirited disposition can infuse a unique energy into romantic connections, but it can also cause instability. Seek to cultivate a sense of focus, despite the many interests competing for your attention. Ensure that your spontaneity doesn't lead to tactless words or reckless actions and is expressed in ways that respect the feelings of others. Learn to appreciate the joys of consistency and commitment, and foster a sense of inner peace in your daily life. Embrace roots and stability, for those are the conditions that hold the greatest promise of happiness in love and life under this challenge.

6

ATTRIBUTES: Nurturing, compassionate, patient, dependable, empathetic, protective, helpful, devoted, responsible, generous, optimistic, harmonious; the consummate parent or caregiver.

PITFALLS:

A tendency to be overprotective can arise from your need to nurture and shelter others; however, sometimes it may be perceived as smothering.

Self-sacrifice, which may cause you to neglect your own needs while prioritizing the needs and wants of others.

Excessive worry can take a toll on you when you stress constantly about the well-being of the people you love.

Resistance to change may arise from a desire for harmony and stability, causing you to adhere to familiar routines, which may repress your personal growth.

Overbearing behavior might occur when your nurturing instincts are perceived by others as controlling or manipulative.

Harboring unrealistic expectations can lead to conflict and disappointment when you expect others to live up to your impossibly high standards.

Martyrdom is a victim behavior you might resort to if you feel unappreciated for your selfless efforts to help others.

Interfering can be a potential pitfall of your keen desire to help others, which may be perceived as meddling.

Intolerance may develop if your strong convictions lead you to harshly judge others.

Perfectionism, rooted in your desire for harmony and balance, is the flip side of your unrealistic standards, which may leave you feeling inadequate or believing others have failed to live up to your lofty expectations.

Dependence could develop if you lean heavily on your mate for validation or to bolster your sense of self-worth, and it could undermine both your confidence and your relationship. Codependent involvements rarely flourish.

YOUR CHALLENGE:

The 6 Transcendent Challenge invites you to find a balance between your nurturing, protective nature and respecting the autonomy of others, especially in romance. Your compassionate and nurturing disposition is a wonderful asset but can tip into overprotectiveness or self-sacrifice if not tempered by restraint. Learn to set healthy boundaries to balance your own needs with your desire to support your partner and others. Embrace change as a natural and necessary part of love and life, even if it feels uncomfortable or threatens your stability. Change isn't always bad, and nothing in life can improve without it.

Temper your expectations in close relationships, and know that no one is perfect. You shouldn't feel disappointed if you expect the impossible and it doesn't happen—after all, it was never possible in the first place! Strive to ensure that as you support your partner, you respect their boundaries and don't come off as smothering or intrusive. Lastly, strive to validate yourself independently of others to augment your sense of self-worth. One sure way to strengthen your relationship is to improve yourself. By addressing these challenges, you can infuse harmony, balance, and depth into your relationships.

7

ATTRIBUTES: Logical, analytical, objective, reasonable, wise, insightful, perceptive, critical thinker, deep thinker, discerning, ethical, emotionally sensitive, spiritually aware, introspective, self-reliant, independent.

PITFALLS:

Detachment is a state that may occur when you become excessively introspective, dwell on your inner feelings, or withdraw from others, potentially impacting your relationships.

Pessimism can manifest when you use your powers of analysis to pick apart a person, a relationship, or a condition in your life, and you fixate on the negative aspects.

Skepticism can emerge when you find yourself consistently doubting or questioning the motives and actions of your partner or other important people in your life.

Cynicism can evolve from being frequently skeptical or overly critical, which may develop into an unhealthy distrust of others' intentions.

Aloofness may develop when your introspection leads others to perceive you as distant or unapproachable.

Over-analysis can lead to unnecessary complications when you over-think or excessively scrutinize a person or situation.

Intolerance can be a potential consequence of critical thinking when you judge others too harshly.

Social withdrawal can stem from a preference for solitude and may contribute to a lack of social interaction and loneliness.

Inflexibility may develop when your precise, analytical nature makes you resistant to change or new ideas.

Isolation is a state that may occur when you withdraw from social interaction, preferring your own company and solitude to such an extreme that leaves you feeling cut off and lonely.

Secretiveness may become a problem when you are feeling emotionally overwhelmed, and it can sow seeds of dishonesty, infidelity, and broken relationships if not checked early on.

YOUR CHALLENGE:

The 7 Transcendent Challenge invites you to utilize the power of analytical thinking and your innate spirituality to maintain emotional balance and channel your feelings into constructive responses. This multi-faceted challenge can take many forms. If pessimism clouds your thinking, focus on the positive aspects of love and life to replace it with optimism. If you are prone to introspection, embrace your temperament, but don't withdraw from important relationships. Remember that self-analysis can have practical benefits, but over-analysis brews complications, especially in romance. If life has made you skeptical, balance it with trust and openness to foster healthy, loving connections. Avoid cynicism. While you may prefer solitude, it needn't lead to social withdrawal or isolation. Instead, carve out time for meaningful interactions with your partner, as well as friends and family. Being adaptable and open to change will benefit you, both in love and life. Finally, try to be honest and direct in your romances, even when you're feeling overwhelmed, and avoid lashing out or seeking escape through secretive behavior and illicit involvements that you may regret. By overcoming these emotional hurdles, you can enhance your personal growth and deepen your romantic connections, building a road to enduring mutual happiness.

8

ATTRIBUTES: Decisive, determined, grounded, a born leader, reliable, sensible, generous, courageous, motivated, confident, magnanimous, ambitious, result-driven, successful.

PITFALLS:

A domineering personality may surface when your strong leadership capabilities are taken to excess. Your assertiveness may be perceived as overbearing or controlling.

Stubbornness may develop when your firm convictions are challenged and you cling to the status quo, unwilling to consider the ideas or viewpoints of others, or rejecting the possibility that what you believe could be wrong.

Aggressive behavior can erupt when your sense of security is threatened or you're attacked, verbally or otherwise.

Workaholic tendencies may develop when you obsess over work or prioritize ambitions over relationships, health, or other important aspects of daily life.

Impatience can spark frustration and a short temper when your goal-driven personality encounters setbacks or delays. Executing hasty decisions purely to move things forward could be counterproductive, leading to more setbacks and delays.

Holding grudges can become a problem when your ego outshouts your better judgment, and you refuse to forgive and move on.

Hopelessness, or despair, can drag you into a dark place when you fail at an important undertaking. You'll likely find it difficult to shake it off and move on to tackle the next challenge.

Insensitivity can chill your likeability and strain your relationships when you neglect to consider others' feelings.

Over-competitiveness can become a problem when your ambitions fuel manipulative or unscrupulous behavior.

YOUR CHALLENGE:

The 8 Transcendent Challenge invites you to balance your assertive temperament and ambition for success by embracing generosity, fairness, and respect for others. Your leadership qualities may take you far, but you must not allow yourself to be dictatorial or controlling, particularly in love. Avoid falling into the trap of believing that the end justifies the means. Ambition is admirable, but not if you become so fixated on success that you abandon your emotional and spiritual side. Remain open-minded and flexible, control your stubbornness, and remember that true strength includes the ability to show kindness and be forgiving.

In your romantic connections, aim to inspire rather than intimidate, leveraging your intellect and charisma. Avoid impatience, and take the time to enjoy the journey, not just the destination. Maintain humility to avoid being perceived as arrogant. Aim to achieve a healthy work-life balance, and don't allow your ambitions and competitive spirit to compromise your ethics. By addressing these challenges, you can be a true leader while fostering deeper, more meaningful connections, both in romance and professional endeavors.

9

ATTRIBUTES: Compassionate, altruistic, empathic, respectful, kind, idealistic, understanding, intuitive, humanitarian, a good listener, spiritually aware.

PITFALLS:

Being overly idealistic may lead to disillusionment when reality falls short of your expectations.

Escapism might occur when you become introverted and withdraw to avoid emotional confrontations.

Indecisiveness may develop from your desire to know and weigh all sides of an argument, leaving you unable to discern what is right or true.

Naivety can be a problem when your idealism makes you overly trusting of others' intentions. Not everyone you meet is kind, honest, or a spiritually evolved soul.

Passivity, and sometimes passive-aggressive behavior, can develop when you seek to avoid conflicts with loved ones but anger or resentment simmers in your thoughts.

Becoming overwhelmed by the problems of loved ones or the world can leave you depressed and wanting to withdraw.

Neglecting self-care may become a problem when your self-sacrificing nature leads you to prioritize the needs of others over your own.

Pessimism, or cynicism, may develop when you dwell too much on the problems of those around you or the world, and you see no hope that conditions will improve.

Resistance to change might develop when you cling to tradition or the status quo as a way of maintaining your stability, which can leave you unwilling to embrace new ideas.

YOUR CHALLENGE:

The 9 Transcendent Challenge encourages you to balance your lofty ideals and principles with a grounded approach to life and love. Try not to allow your altruism to dampen your optimism when reality falls short of your expectations. Avoid using philosophical or dogmatic excuses, like "I don't deserve anything more," or "That's just how society is." to rationalize vexing predicaments in your life. Don't hesitate to take charge and initiate improvements in your life when they're needed. Strive to express your beliefs without appearing self-righteous or judgmental, and be respectful of opposing viewpoints. Your compassion is admirable, but don't sacrifice yourself to avoid standing up for what you believe or know is right. Defend your integrity, your boundaries, and your comfort zone.

With the 9 challenge, you'll need to find constructive ways to manage your feelings and maintain your stability so that you're not overwhelmed by others' needs or emotions. Prioritize self-care, and remember, it's okay to put your own needs first. You can't help others if you are too depleted to help yourself. Don't allow the burden of caring for others to compromise your well-being. Embrace a positive outlook at all times. In romance, don't let your compassionate nature leave you vulnerable to manipulation or turn you into a victim. Closely examine words, motives, and actions so that you don't fall prey to gullibility or misplaced trust.

Overcoming this challenge may not be easy, as it reflects a failure to grasp the intricacies of deep emotions or the spiritual component in all life throughout the universe. Learning to manage your emotions and avoid leaning into pessimism or despair when life throws you a challenge will be a rewarding first step. This is key to building stronger relationships and deriving more satisfaction from intimacy. You have a keen awareness of your partner's wants and needs, and a boundless reservoir of love and affection to share, but you must remain stable and optimistic to chart a course to happiness.

○

ATTRIBUTES: Evolved, experienced, worldly, independent, intelligent, conscientious, observant, organized, meticulous, principled, unattached.

PITFALLS:

Detachment can occur when you lose interest in the world or believe you've done and seen everything life has to offer, and there's nothing left for you to learn.

Apathy can develop when daily activities and relationships no longer bring you joy or fulfillment.

A cold, callous, or cruel disposition can take root when you experience disappointment or defeat in an undertaking and you become hopeless or believe your life is meaningless.

Isolation may set in when you lose sight of your purpose or meaning in life, and one way this can manifest is resentment, often unfounded, directed at friends or loved ones.

Hypercriticism can occur when you judge others harshly or express disappointment when they fail to meet your high standards, alienating those you care about and injecting discord into your relationships.

Animosity, or malice, can bubble up when you obsess over former lovers or friends who have broken your trust as well as those who have committed perceived slights against you.

A manipulative or controlling demeanor can emerge when your imagination runs wild, and you fear people you trust are working against you.

YOUR CHALLENGE:

The 0 Transcendent Challenge is unique and rarely found in numerology charts. It reflects a fundamental need to become more interested and invested in the world around you. While you may feel that you've seen and done all life has to offer, realize that every day can bring new experiences. Don't allow apathy or detachment to take root in your emotional landscape. The best defense against this is to seek active engagement with others. Share their emotions and experiences. Embrace life with the knowledge that each day brings a new panoply of challenges and adventures. Avoid hypercritical behavior that may alienate people you care about, and cultivate empathy and tolerance. Strive to build grounded, meaningful relationships with people who share your interests and life goals. Keep a check on your ego or perceived arrogance by reminding yourself that we all have room for growth and self-improvement. Although you have no karmic lessons, your challenge lies in maintaining your sense of humanity and active engagement with friends, family, romantic partners, and the world around you.

Chapter 8
Evaluating Your Relationships

Assuming that you've followed the guidelines given in Chapter 2 for crafting your numerology love chart and delved into the relevant interpretations, you should now possess a wealth of insights on your desires, attributes, pitfalls, and trends shaping your romantic prospects. Similarly, by utilizing the same numerological tools, you should have gleaned the same valuable insights into your partner or a potential lover's intimate character.

Having covered the essentials, we now advance to the next significant step in your pursuit of romantic fulfillment: the evaluation of your relationships. This intriguing facet of numerology may be useful to those considering a new commitment as well as those currently in a relationship. It will enable you to evaluate a potential partner's compatibility at a glance across every relevant level—emotional, sexual, and karmic. By utilizing a series of straightforward techniques, you can easily evaluate the strengths and weaknesses of any relationship, scrutinize subtle influences at work in daily life, and even predict the long-term viability of a love affair.

The challenge of identifying compatible partners from the vast spectrum of possible candidates has been an ongoing quest since the beginning of time. Romantic disappointments often occur because we overlook minor incompatibilities and nuances between personalities and temperaments. It's all too easy to become so infatuated with the initial fervor of a romance or a captivating lover's physical allure that we fail to recognize warning signs of incompatibility, only for them to grow into significant minefields later. Even when we strive to realistically assess a new partner or a budding involvement, identifying incongruous personalities or behaviors may be impossible without first establishing a relationship. But once involved, we are left to find out the hard way.

Consequently, many people stumble into relationships, unsure if they are even somewhat compatible with newfound mates. Most of us have made this mistake, and some continue to repeat it. We get involved, optimistically hoping for the best, but encounter disappointment and romantic failure because of poor judgment. Commonly known as "learning the hard way," this haphazard approach is just that: a risky, often painful experiment that more often than not leads to disillusionment in love and sex rather than bliss.

Numerology doesn't offer any mystical secrets for evaluating compatibility, but it does suggest a more rational approach—one that eliminates the guesswork and improves the odds of a forging successful, satisfying relationship.

In this chapter, you will learn how to perform detailed comparisons for current and potential relationships. You'll discover methods for evaluating the temperament of partners, as well as procedures for determining your emotional, mental, and sexual compatibility, or lack thereof. You will also learn how to predict the longevity of a relationship. Regardless of your current situation, numerology can offer you insightful perspectives on your romantic landscape, helping you navigate the emotional wilderness.

How To Begin

To undertake intimate comparisons, we are concerned with four aspects in a numerology chart: Love Vibration, Romantic Destiny, Sexual Consensus, and Karma. Each aspect must be carefully evaluated on its own, and then in combination with other components in your chart, then your partner's chart, and finally, both charts side by side before drawing any conclusions.

The initial step of the evaluation process involves your Love Vibration. Here, you compare your strengths, weaknesses, desires, and overall temperament with those of your partner. This numerological technique enables you to gauge your emotional compatibility at a glance. You can discover whether your Love Vibrations, when considered together, point to a harmonious relationship or one likely to encounter significant downsides and potential discord.

The second step in evaluating compatibility involves analyzing your Romantic Destiny trend. Comparing this aspect in your love chart with your partner's Romantic Destiny will reveal whether the two of you will travel similar or disparate life paths, and from this, you can discern an accurate indication of your prospects for an enduring relationship. It can also provide useful insights into the numerological vibrations working for and against your relationship as time goes by.

The third step in this process involves analyzing your Sexual Consensus. Again, we compare this aspect in your chart with your partner's Sexual Consensus vibration. Physical intimacy plays a crucial role in nearly every romance, and by carefully examining your interaction on this level, you can discover whether you are sexually compatible. Likewise, potential conflicts can be identified and a clear picture formed of the shortcomings and pitfalls that lurk in the physical side of your relationship.

The fourth and final step discussed in this chapter pertains to your karmic compatibility. With this numerological method, you can gauge your compatibility with a partner on the spiritual, or subconscious, level, analyzing qualities that are often subtle but commonly to blame for romantic discord and failure.

To perform your first compatibility analysis, work through the instructions given below. Before long, with familiarity and practice, you'll be able to chart comprehensive numerological analyses for your romantic affairs with precision and ease, gleaning insights that you can use to enhance your love life and fortify your relationships.

Explanation

Before attempting to perform numerological analyses, you should understand that compatibility—whether emotional, intellectual, or sexual—cannot be broadly defined by a simple "yes, you're compatible" or "no, you're not" answer. Instead, it is nuanced and measured by degree. Numerologists recognize that certain vibrations are harmonious, while others are more or less compatible, or entirely incompatible. Vibrations interact according to natural principles, which a numerologist can accurately chart and observe. When comparing two love charts, we aim to pinpoint the level of compatibility, the strengths of a relationship, and potential pitfalls that might be encountered along the way.

For this chapter, we'll be working with the nine primary vibrations (1-9) and the five master vibrations (11, 14, 16, 19, and 22). Depending on how individuals attuned to these vibrations interact, we classify the degree of compatibility into five distinct ratings: cardinal, mutable, complementary, fixed, and polar. A summary of each assessment follows.

Cardinal: When two vibrations ideally harmonize, we refer to them as *cardinal* vibrations. This interaction is particularly auspicious in romance. When two cardinal vibrations unite, the ideal love affair may blossom. Numerologists often refer to these partners as "soul mates." Their personalities are highly compatible, and they complement each other's attributes and shortcomings, bringing out the best in both. This pairing promises the best chance for profound, enduring happiness in love and marriage.

Mutable: Vibrations that are not 100% compatible but generally align and interact favorably are categorized as *mutable* vibrations. Relationships based on mutable vibrations are often successful. While compatibility is fairly high, partners with mutable vibrations are not always well attuned, and contrasting temperaments may cause friction. However, these individuals usually have a solid understanding of each other and can make any adjustments, usually minor, required to ensure a satisfying relationship. Generally, the pitfalls found in these pairings are relatively minor, and the obstacles hindering fulfillment are few.

Complementary: Two partners imbued with very similar temperaments might understand each other well, but that doesn't mean they're compatible. In some respects, they might be badly matched. We classify such pairings of two very similar vibrations as *complementary*. These pairings usually favor brief romances, and connections could be intense and satisfying but not very stable. Lasting commitments or marriage might not be favored. In romance, these partners understand one another as well as they understand themselves, but that isn't always advantageous. The likelihood of mutual satisfaction is strong, but significant headwinds could arise. Most of these relationships will become unsatisfying and dysfunctional unless both partners compromise, cooperate, and invest considerable effort to preserve stability. Another potential downside is that partners in complementary pairings might accentuate each other's positive traits but also amplify their weaknesses and draw out their negative qualities. If not kept in check, this could impact a relationship in numerous detrimental ways.

Fixed: Two vibrations that have more dissimilar qualities than similar ones are referred to as *fixed* vibrations. Lovers in these pairings probably have little in common. Personality differences are glaring, often prompting onlookers to wonder, "Why are these two together?" An inability to comprehend each other's feelings and temperament may fuel constant friction and misunderstandings. Alternatively, too much similarity in the wrong areas, such as shared negative traits, may provoke tension and strife. In some cases, lovers with fixed vibrations may find themselves at odds yet refuse to compromise. Fixed combinations can be stable but are more apt to be a source of discord unless both partners make a concerted effort to identify the shortcomings in their relationship and strive for a more tolerant, patient approach to these differences when they arise. Of utmost importance, both must be willing to yield when necessary.

Polar: In instances where two vibrations are opposite, and the partner's personalities will probably be opposite as well, numerologists classify these pairings as *polar* vibrations. These relationships can be exciting and intense, but they're almost always unstable. Long-term commitments are unlikely. The partners have nothing in common, which can be mutually intriguing at the start, but as the relationship develops, it may quickly become volatile, marred by arguments and discord, and prone to mutual self-destruction in some cases. These lovers will find it difficult or impossible to reconcile their differences, and neither may be motivated to do so. Despite the downsides, if both individuals make an unwavering commitment to stability and keep the lines of communication open between them, happiness in romance might, in some cases, be possible.

Evaluating Emotional Compatibility

The Love Vibration analysis evaluates the degree of emotional compatibility between two partners. To arrive at this analysis, we compare the Love Vibration in your love chart with your partner's Love Vibration using the following procedure:

1) Refer to your numerology chart for your Love Vibration, assuming you've followed the steps given earlier in Chapter 2. If not, refer to Step #1 in Chapter 2 and calculate this value now. Do the same for your partner or prospective mate. Note that you

can use this method to evaluate your emotional compatibility with friends, family, colleagues, and others.

2) Consult the Comparison Tables below. These tables are labeled in the upper left corner with the primary and master numbers. Locate the table applicable to your Love Vibration and look under the column corresponding to your gender. Then, read across to find your partner's Love Vibration. An evaluation is shown in the left column, indicating whether your Love Vibration pairing is cardinal, mutable, complementary, fixed, or polar.

3) Refer back to the definitions of cardinal, mutable, complementary, fixed, and polar earlier in this chapter for an interpretation of your assessment. As a quick reminder, these terms refer to the level of emotional compatibility between the numerological vibrations: "Cardinal" is ideal compatibility, "mutable" indicates general alignment, "complementary" suggests similar temperaments but potential mismatches, "fixed" warns of significant differences, and "polar" indicates opposite and typically incompatible vibrations.

4) Record the applicable interpretation in your love chart for future reference. This will allow you to compare and contrast the results of this analysis with other aspects in your love chart as you proceed through these steps.

5) Once you've completed this assessment, proceed to the next step in the evaluation process.

LOVE VIBRATION COMPATIBILITY TABLES

1 Vibration	Male	Female
Cardinal	3, 6, 19	3, 8, 14
Mutable	8, 11, 16	11, 19, 22
Complementary	1, 2, 14	1, 5, 16
Fixed	5, 7, 22	2, 6, 7
Polar	4, 9	4, 9

2 Vibration	Male	Female
Cardinal	6, 9, 16	6, 8, 16
Mutable	4, 8, 11	4, 11, 22
Complementary	3, 7, 19	1, 3, 7
Fixed	1, 2, 22	2, 9, 19
Polar	5, 14	5, 14

3 Vibration	Male	Female
Cardinal	1, 11, 19	1, 11, 19
Mutable	5, 6, 9	8, 14, 16
Complementary	2, 4, 14	2, 5, 6
Fixed	3, 8, 16	3, 4, 22
Polar	7, 22	7, 9

4 Vibration	Male	Female
Cardinal	4, 7, 22	4, 7, 8
Mutable	2, 6, 8	2, 6, 22
Complementary	9, 11, 19	3, 5, 11
Fixed	3, 5, 16	9, 14, 16
Polar	1, 14	1, 19

5 Vibration	Male	Female
Cardinal	8, 14, 19	14, 19, 22
Mutable	6, 16, 22	3, 8, 11
Complementary	1, 3, 4	7, 9, 16
Fixed	5, 7, 9	1, 4, 5
Polar	2, 11	2, 6

6 Vibration	Male	Female
Cardinal	2, 6, 22	1, 2, 6
Mutable	4, 9, 19	3, 4, 5
Complementary	3, 8, 11	8, 11, 19
Fixed	1, 7, 14	7, 9, 22
Polar	5, 16	14, 16

7 Vibration	Male	Female
Cardinal	4, 7, 22	4, 7, 22
Mutable	9, 14, 19	11, 14, 16
Complementary	2, 5, 8	3, 8, 9
Fixed	1, 6, 11	1, 5, 6
Polar	3, 16	3, 19

8 Vibration	Male	Female
Cardinal	1, 2, 4	5, 14, 19
Mutable	3, 5, 11	1, 2, 4
Complementary	6, 7, 16	6, 7, 9
Fixed	8, 14, 22	3, 8, 22
Polar	9, 19	11, 16

9 Vibration	Male	Female
Cardinal	9, 14, 16	2, 9, 22
Mutable	11, 19, 22	3, 6, 7
Complementary	5, 7, 8	4, 11, 14
Fixed	2, 4, 6	5, 16, 19
Polar	1, 3	1, 8

11 Vibration	Male	Female
Cardinal	3, 11, 16	3, 11, 16
Mutable	1, 2, 5, 7	1, 2, 8, 9
Complementary	2, 6, 9	4, 6
Fixed	14, 22	7, 14, 19
Polar	8, 19	5, 22

14 Vibration	Male	Female
Cardinal	1, 5, 8	5, 9, 16
Mutable	3, 7, 22	7, 19, 22
Complementary	9, 14, 19	1, 3, 14
Fixed	4, 11, 16	6, 8, 11
Polar	2, 6	2, 4

16 Vibration	Male	Female
Cardinal	2, 11, 14, 16	2, 9, 11, 16
Mutable	3, 7	1, 5
Complementary	1, 5, 22	8, 19, 22
Fixed	4, 9, 19	3, 4, 14
Polar	6, 8	6, 7

19 Vibration	Male	Female
Cardinal	3, 5, 8	1, 3, 5
Mutable	1, 14	6, 7, 9
Complementary	6, 16, 19, 22	2, 4, 14
Fixed	2, 9, 11	16, 19, 22
Polar	4, 7	8, 11

22 Vibration	Male	Female
Cardinal	5, 7, 9	4, 6, 7
Mutable	1, 2, 4, 14	5, 9, 14
Complementary	16	16, 19
Fixed	3, 6, 8, 19	1, 2, 8, 11
Polar	11, 22	3, 22

Forecasting Future Compatibility

The second step in intimate comparisons involves analyzing the Romantic Destiny vibrations. This provides insights into the long-term potential of any relationship, indicating whether your life path aligns or conflicts with your partner. For this assessment, we are concerned with three possible outcomes: cardinal, mutable, and fixed. For our purposes here, these terms have similar meanings to what was given previously, and the specific definitions are explained here:

Cardinal: Partners who share cardinal Romantic Destiny vibrations are most likely to achieve lasting happiness. Their life paths align harmoniously, and their joys and sorrows will be shared. Serious obstacles rarely occur, and unless other aspects of the partners' love chart reflect instability, they can expect enduring compatibility of interests, goals, and temperaments.

Mutable: Partners who share mutable Romantic Destiny vibrations are mostly in sync. Their life paths are not identical but compatible enough to take them in the same general direction. Enduring romantic bliss and a wealth of shared life experiences are possible, as long as minor everyday events are not blown out of proportion and allowed to undermine the stability of the relationship.

Fixed: Partners with fixed Romantic Destiny vibrations may face many pressures arising from their divergent paths. Both individuals are firmly committed to their own life goals, making compromise difficult. Competing or diverging interests may eventually draw them to opposite paths. Fixed pairings are considered the least favorable, but romance or marriage should not be ruled out if there's sufficient love, a mutual spirit of cooperation, and the willingness to work through difficulties.

To perform this analysis, follow these steps:

1. If you've followed the instructions given in Chapter 2, refer to your numerology chart to find your Romantic Destiny vibration; otherwise, calculate this value now using Step #2 in Chapter 2. Do the same for your mate or a potential partner.

2. Consult the Destiny Trend Analysis Key below. Find your Romantic Destiny vibration in the left column, then move across that row to the column that corresponds to your partner's Romantic Destiny vibration. The possible values in the table are C (for cardinal), M (for mutable), and F (for fixed).

DESTINY TREND ANALYSIS KEY

	1	2	3	4	5	6	7	8	9	11	14	16	19	22
1	C	F	C	F	C	M	F	M	M	C	M	M	C	C
2	M	C	M	F	F	C	M	C	M	M	F	C	C	F
3	C	M	C	F	C	F	F	M	F	C	C	M	M	F
4	F	C	F	C	M	M	C	C	M	M	F	F	M	C
5	M	F	M	M	C	F	F	M	F	C	C	C	C	M
6	M	M	M	C	F	C	M	C	F	M	F	C	C	F
7	F	M	F	C	F	M	C	C	C	M	M	M	F	C
8	C	M	M	M	M	F	M	C	F	C	C	F	C	F
9	F	C	F	C	F	C	C	F	C	M	F	M	M	C
11	M	F	C	M	M	M	M	F	C	C	M	F	F	M
14	C	F	M	F	C	F	M	F	M	F	C	C	M	F
16	M	C	C	M	M	C	C	F	M	M	M	C	F	F
19	C	M	C	M	C	M	F	M	M	F	C	F	C	C
22	F	M	F	C	M	C	C	M	M	F	F	F	C	C

3. Record the applicable interpretation in your love chart for future reference.

4. Once you have ascertained your Romantic Destiny compatibility rating, proceed to the next step.

Evaluating Sexual Compatibility

The process for evaluating sexual compatibility using numerology is similar to the one just described for emotional analysis, except it's based on the Sexual Consensus vibration rather than the Love vibration. The five compatibility ratings (cardinal, mutable, complementary, fixed, and polar) and their meanings remain the same. The comparison tables below have the same format as the ones used for the Love Vibration analysis.

To evaluate your sexual compatibility with a mate or prospective lover, follow these steps:

1) If you've calculated your numerology chart as directed in Chapter 2, look up your Sexual Consensus vibration. If not, calculate this value now using Step #4 in Chapter 2, and repeat this procedure for your mate or potential partner.

2) Consult the Comparison Tables below. The tables are labeled with the primary and master numbers in the upper left corner. Look in the column corresponding to your gender and then locate your partner's Sexual Consensus vibration. Your assessment is shown in the left column. As a reminder, "cardinal" reflects ideal compatibility, "mutable" implies a general alignment, "complementary" vibrations are similar but potentially mismatched, "fixed" implies significant differences, and "polar" refers to opposite, incompatible vibrations.

3) Record the results for this comparison in your love chart for future reference.

4) Once you've completed this assessment, proceed to the next step in the compatibility analysis.

SEXUAL CONSENSUS COMPARISON GUIDE

1 Vibration	Male	Female
Cardinal	1, 4, 14	1, 3, 11
Mutable	5, 6, 11, 16	5, 14, 19
Complementary	8, 19	8, 9, 16
Fixed	2, 4, 7	2, 6, 22
Polar	9, 22	4, 7

2 Vibration	Male	Female
Cardinal	2, 6, 9	2, 8, 16
Mutable	8, 16, 19	6, 9, 11
Complementary	4, 7, 22	3, 7, 19
Fixed	1, 3, 11	1, 4, 22
Polar	5, 14	5, 14

3 Vibration	Male	Female
Cardinal	1, 5, 14	1, 11, 19
Mutable	3, 11, 19	3, 5, 14
Complementary	2, 8, 16	6, 8, 16
Fixed	6, 9, 22	2, 4, 7
Polar	4, 7	9, 22

4 Vibration	Male	Female
Cardinal	4, 7, 22	4, 8, 22
Mutable	6, 8, 9	6, 7, 8
Complementary	11, 14, 19	2, 11, 14
Fixed	2, 3, 5	1, 5, 16
Polar	1, 16	3, 19

5 Vibration	Male	Female
Cardinal	5, 14, 19	3, 5, 14
Mutable	1, 3, 11	1, 8, 19
Complementary	6, 8, 16	9, 16, 22
Fixed	4, 9, 22	4, 6, 11
Polar	2, 7	2, 7

6 Vibration	Male	Female
Cardinal	6, 9, 22	2, 6, 8
Mutable	2, 4, 16	1, 4, 9
Complementary	3, 7, 11	5, 7, 11
Fixed	1, 5, 8	3, 16, 19
Polar	14, 19	14, 22

7 Vibration	Male	Female
Cardinal	7, 9, 16	4, 7, 9
Mutable	4, 8, 22	8, 16, 22
Complementary	2, 6, 11	2, 6, 11
Fixed	3, 14, 19	1, 14, 19
Polar	1, 5	3, 5

8 Vibration	Male	Female
Cardinal	2, 4, 6	11, 19, 22
Mutable	5, 7, 22	2, 4, 7
Complementary	1, 3, 14	1, 3, 5
Fixed	9, 16, 19	6, 9, 14
Polar	8, 11	8, 16

9 Vibration	Male	Female
Cardinal	7, 11, 22	2, 6, 7
Mutable	2, 4, 6	4, 11, 16
Complementary	1, 5, 9	9, 14, 22
Fixed	8, 14, 16	3, 5, 8
Polar	3, 19	1, 19

11 Vibration	Male	Female
Cardinal	1, 3, 8	9, 16, 19
Mutable	2, 9, 14	1, 3, 5
Complementary	4, 6, 7	4, 6, 7
Fixed	5, 16, 19	2, 14, 22
Polar	11, 22	8, 11

14 Vibration	Male	Female
Cardinal	5, 16, 19	1, 3, 5
Mutable	1, 3, 14	11, 14, 22
Complementary	4, 9, 22	4, 8, 19
Fixed	7, 8, 11	7, 9, 16
Polar	2, 6	2, 6

16 Vibration	Male	Female
Cardinal	2, 11, 19	7, 14, 22
Mutable	7, 9, 22	1, 2, 6
Complementary	1, 3, 5	3, 5, 19
Fixed	4, 6, 14	8, 9, 11
Polar	8, 16	4, 16

19 Vibration	Male	Female
Cardinal	3, 8, 11	5, 14, 16
Mutable	1, 5, 19	2, 3, 19
Complementary	2, 14, 16	1, 4, 22
Fixed	6, 7, 22	7, 8, 11
Polar	4, 9	6, 9

22 Vibration	Male	Female
Cardinal	4, 8, 16	4, 6, 9
Mutable	7, 14, 22	7, 8, 16, 22
Complementary	5, 9, 19	2, 14
Fixed	1, 2, 11	3, 5, 19
Polar	3, 6	1, 11

Evaluating Transcendent Challenge Compatibility

The final step in numerological analysis examines the Transcendent Challenge vibration for each partner and assesses whether their attributes and pitfalls are compatible. Some numerologists refer to this component as "Personality Compatibility" since it analyzes the partners' character traits, pitfalls, and challenges they must overcome to express their positive qualities in daily life. By comparing the Transcendent Challenge vibrations, we can predict their prospects for harmonious interaction. We can also identify and analyze subconscious attitudes and behavioral tendencies that may work for and against emotional and physical intimacy.

For this numerological aspect, four ratings are possible:

Compatible: In a "Compatible" pairing, both partners' inherent strengths, weaknesses, and challenges are in harmony. They are likely to understand and empathize with each other's daily struggles and growth points. Their aligned challenges promote mutual growth and support. They will be able to face their challenges together, provide support to one another, and encourage personal development.

Workable: A "Workable" pairing requires some effort to achieve or maintain compatibility. These partners may have unrelated challenges, but they are complementary. While their struggles and growth points might not be fully in sync, they provide opportunities for personal growth, as long as both partners are willing to invest the effort. With patience, empathy, and mutual respect, they can work through their challenges.

Difficult: This pairing reflects significant disparities in both partners' life challenges. Their differences could spark misunderstandings or conflict, and both partners may struggle to be empathetic or support one another's growth paths. Despite the difficulties, couples can overcome these hurdles and achieve happiness and permanence in love, but it will require considerable effort, patience, and cooperation.

Incompatible: An "Incompatible" rating forewarns that the life challenges faced by these partners are so disparate that they may struggle greatly to empathize with and support each other in daily life. Disagreements and discord are likely and may be difficult to resolve. Even in the face of such challenges, however, remember that all relationships require work. Seemingly incompatible partners may be able to establish strong, enduring bonds when there is sufficient desire and effort invested into the relationship.

Remember, in numerology, these ratings represent just one aspect of overall compatibility and should be interpreted in context with the other aspects in each individual's chart. Despite apparent incompatibility, any relationship can succeed if both partners are willing to support one another and work to find constructive solutions to problems as they arise.

To deduce your level of personality compatibility with your mate or a potential partner, follow these steps:

1) If you have calculated your love chart as directed earlier in Chapter 2, look up the Transcendent Challenge vibration for yourself and your mate or any potential partner. If not, calculate your Transcendent Challenge using Step #5 in Chapter 2, and then do the same for your partner.

2) Refer to the Transcendent Challenge Evaluation Tables below. The first column corresponds to your own Transcendent Challenge vibration, the second to your partner's, and the third provides the compatibility assessment. To use the table, find your Challenge vibration in the first column, find your partner's Challenge vibration in the second column, and read across to see the assessment.

3) Record the result of this comparison in your love chart for future reference and to allow comparisons and analysis with other sections or other partners' numerology charts.

Transcendent Challenge Evaluation Tables

Your Challenge	Partner's Challenge	Evaluation
1	3, 5, 9	Compatible
	1, 7, 0	Workable
	2, 4, 6	Challenging
	8	Incompatible

Your Challenge	Partner's Challenge	Evaluation
2	4, 6, 0	Compatible
	2, 8	Workable
	1, 3, 5	Challenging
	7, 9	Incompatible

Your Challenge	Partner's Challenge	Evaluation
3	1, 7, 9	Compatible
	3, 0	Workable
	2, 4, 8	Challenging
	5, 6	Incompatible

Your Challenge	Partner's Challenge	Evaluation
4	2, 6, 8	Compatible
	4, 9	Workable
	1, 3, 5, 0	Challenging
	7	Incompatible

Your Challenge	Partner's Challenge	Evaluation
5	1, 7, 0	Compatible
	5, 9	Workable
	2, 4, 6, 8	Challenging
	3	Incompatible

Your Challenge	Partner's Challenge	Evaluation
6	2, 4, 0	Compatible
	6, 8	Workable
	1, 3, 5, 9	Challenging
	7	Incompatible

Your Challenge	Partner's Challenge	Evaluation
7	1, 3, 5, 9	Compatible
	7	Workable
	2, 4, 6	Challenging
	8	Incompatible

Your Challenge	Partner's Challenge	Evaluation
8	2, 4, 6	Compatible
	8, 0	Workable
	1, 3, 5, 9	Challenging
	7	Incompatible

Your Challenge	Partner's Challenge	Evaluation
9	1, 3, 5, 7	Compatible
	4, 9	Workable
	2, 6, 8	Challenging
	0	Incompatible

Your Challenge	Partner's Challenge	Evaluation
0	2, 6, 8	Compatible
	1, 3, 5, 7, 9	Workable
	0	Challenging
	4	Incompatible

A Final Thought

The techniques and interpretive guidelines in this chapter represent one of several systems widely used by numerologists to evaluate intimate relationships. This method is easy to master and offers an accuracy level that rivals other more complex, time-consuming techniques. The charts and tables presented above are designed to provide quick, understandable interpretations for convenience.

If you find yourself unsure about the rating for a particular aspect, or if you desire a more in-depth analysis of any individual or relationship, refer back to the earlier chapters. Review the meanings for the specific aspect, first individually, then in comparison. For instance, if you have questions about the Love Vibration analysis, consult the chapter that deals with that aspect of the love chart and review the corresponding passages. Perform systematic comparisons, point-by-point, until you can draw logical conclusions. Consider the strengths and weaknesses, desires, attitudes, and habits as well as the potential pitfalls of the vibration pairing being considered.

Chapter 9
Assessing Your Emotional Interaction

What happens if you find yourself bogged down in an unhappy marriage, or if a meaningful love affair is teetering on the brink of failure? Is it possible to attain shared satisfaction and joy when your numerological compatibility, as discussed in the previous chapter, appears unfavorable? Can numerology suggest proactive steps couples might take to alleviate conflict and improve their interactions?

These are questions commonly asked by those seeking to mend troubled relationships. Often, people feel powerless in the face of intimate crises or failure, standing by as their romances crumble and blaming the collapse on external factors. Most of the time, once a love affair breaks down, our power to rectify the situation is lost.

Fortunately, there are identifiable actions you can take to forestall heartbreak and romantic failure. Imagine you are in a committed relationship that lacks the fulfilling qualities you and your partner desire. Perhaps constant arguments consume your time together, or you barely experience the joys of deep intimacy. Maybe your personalities are either too competitive or too alike. You could:

(a) continue pursuing your current path and hope your relationship will improve on its own;

(b) seek professional relationship counseling;

(c) opt for separation or divorce and walk away; or,

(d) use numerology to identify specific incompatibilities in your relationship and proactively address those issues.

The fourth option—utilizing the science of numerology to effect positive change in your love life—can reveal a pathway to fine-tune your relationships and achieve romantic bliss. This chapter explains how you can seize this opportunity.

In numerology, we recognize that certain relationships are more likely to succeed than others, and we can discern clear evidence of why that is so. We can identify vibrations and trends in a love chart working for and against a relationship without our being aware of it. For instance, two partners who share cardinal vibrations in key aspects of their love chart are far more likely to succeed than a couple with polar extremes who will face a daily panoply of misunderstandings and discord.

Over decades, I have analyzed thousands of numerology charts for couples, young and old, across a wide range of temperaments. Some charts revealed minor incompatibilities with clear solutions. Others indicated severe incompatibilities that were undermining their intimacy. Some couples had tried a variety of methods to resolve their conflicts with little or no success. However, numerology has offered consistently useful insights allowing countless couples to reimagine dramatic improvements in their relationships.

Numerology employs a precise and accurate method, known as "Interactive Analysis," to provide deep insights into any love affair or marriage. With this technique, couples can identify concrete actions they can take to effect positive change in their day-to-day interaction. The methods discussed in this chapter draw upon the tools used in Interactive Analysis to restore harmony, boost compatibility, and enhance one-on-one communication on every level. These methods can pinpoint potential sources of friction and reinforce harmony and stability before a relationship begins to deteriorate. Even romances marred by sexual incompatibility, conflicting desires, or infidelity can be rehabilitated.

How Numerology Can Work for You

With Interactive Analysis, a numerologist (or you) can identify a spectrum of distinct personality traits that can affect intimacy. These include strengths, weaknesses, attitudes, and habits. Thanks to these useful insights, it is possible to identify and analyze the many subtle influences working for and against a relationship.

Numerologists use two distinct charts for this process: the "Emotional Interaction Profile" and the "Sexual Interaction Profile." A sample of the first type of chart is shown here:

EMOTIONAL INTERACTION PROFILE

Behavioral Compatibility (Assertive/Passive)		
You	Your Partner	Assessment

Self-Confidence Compatibility (Secure/Insecure)		
You	Your Partner	Assessment

Extroversion Compatibility (Extroverted/Introverted)		
You	Your Partner	Assessment

Reactivity Compatibility (Stable/Impulsive)		
You	Your Partner	Assessment

Agreeableness Compatibility (Cooperative/Stubborn)		
You	Your Partner	Assessment

Blank templates for both chart formats are provided at the end of this book. You can use these for the steps outlined below or make photocopies. Alternatively, you can keep notebook paper handy to write down your compatibility evaluations.

The methodologies and interpretive guidelines utilized for Interactive Analysis are detailed below. For the best outcomes, follow all instructions in the order given, progressing from one step to the next. Analyze each result to understand how it might be impacting your relationship before going on to the next.

To begin an assessment of your Emotional Interaction, you must know your Love Vibration and your partner's. If you have not yet computed your basic numerology chart, refer to Chapter 2 and follow the instructions for Step #1. Once you know both Love Vibrations, you can move forward.

Determining Behavioral Compatibility

Consult the table below and locate your Love Vibration in the column corresponding to your gender. Read across to the right column, labeled "Behavioral Assessment," and note your rating in your Emotional Interaction Profile or on paper. Repeat this step for your mate or any potential partner.

Male	Female	Behavioral Assessment
1, 5, 8, 14, 19	1, 5, 8, 14, 16	Very Assertive
3, 6, 7, 11, 16	3, 4, 7, 11, 19	Moderately Assertive
2, 4, 9, 22	2, 6, 9, 22	Passive

Refer to the next table, labeled "Behavioral Compatibility," for an assessment of this trait, which will be either "Favorable" or "Potentially Difficult." Write down this assessment in your Emotional Interaction Profile.

Review the interpretations following the table to learn how your Behavioral Compatibility assessment could be impacting your relationship.

Your Assessment	Your Partner	Behavioral Compatibility
Very Assertive	*Very Assertive*	Potentially Difficult
Very Assertive	*Moderately Assertive*	Favorable
Very Assertive	*Passive*	Potentially Difficult
Moderately Assertive	*Very Assertive*	Favorable
Moderately Assertive	*Moderately Assertive*	Favorable
Moderately Assertive	*Passive*	Favorable
Passive	*Very Assertive*	Potentially Difficult
Passive	*Moderately Assertive*	Favorable
Passive	*Passive*	Potentially Difficult

Favorable: If this assessment applies to your relationship, it enhances your emotional compatibility. You and your partner understand how to share the lead without competing or struggling to impose your will or views on each other. You know when to compromise, and you can do so without provoking stress or misunderstandings. As long as you both use common sense and embrace a spirit of cooperation, this positive quality will work to promote deep, enduring happiness.

Potentially Difficult: If this assessment applies to your relationship, you and your partner may be able to work out your differences while maintaining calm, harmonious interaction. However, many couples find it difficult to make the necessary adjustments to achieve or restore a fulfilling relationship. Understanding the common pitfalls and remedies associated with the following variations of this pairing may prove helpful.

Two partners who are both very assertive: Frequent arguments, hostility, and lack of cooperation are the main pitfalls in this relationship. Both partners may struggle to keep the dominant role, imposing their likes and dislikes on the other. This can result in anger and upheaval. One or both individuals might dwell on past disagreements or deliberately offend the other in an attempt to provoke and throw them off balance. If this conflicting interaction persists, it will be hard to prevent romantic failure.

Highly assertive partners must rein in their dominant instincts and learn to compromise. Alternating the dominant role from one partner to the other, and focusing on aspects of the relationship where compatibility does exist, can preserve a harmonious relationship. When one partner resists making positive changes, the other should take the initiative, avoiding conflict and assuming a more flexible role. Stubborn mates may respond favorably with surprising reciprocity, and if not, it may be necessary to take a closer look at whether the love affair is worth maintaining.

One partner is more assertive than the other: Typically, the less assertive partner ends up at a disadvantage in this relationship, especially if they are frequently forced into a passive or submissive role. Hypersensitivity, depression, and reduced confidence may arise from a sense of being bullied, abused, or taken for granted. Eventually, the individual might lash out in resentment at the dominant partner or resort to impulsive behavior or infidelity to escape their unhappiness. A lover unwillingly forced into a passive role should consider terminating the relationship if it is burdensome or oppressive.

To strengthen or restore harmonious interaction, the more assertive partner must make a concerted effort to develop self-control and tolerance, while the more passive individual must be willing to accept new responsibilities and stand up as an equal. Should the dominant individual fail to perceive the need for such improvement, candid discussion could open the door to change. If the person still takes no interest in improving the relationship, it will probably continue on the same unhappy path indefinitely, and its value should be carefully re-examined.

Two partners who are passive: Confusion, instability, and resentment typically plague lovers in this kind of relationship. Passive individuals rarely exhibit assertive qualities and expect their partners to take the initiative. When neither individual wants to lead, the relationship bogs down in confusion and uncertainty. Alternatively, boredom and monotony could befall one or both partners due to a lack of stimulating interaction.

To enhance the chances of enduring happiness, both partners must consciously acknowledge the problem, and one or both should be willing to assume a more assertive role. One practical approach to resolution might be for both to agree to switch the onus of being assertive from one partner to the other every few weeks or every month or two. In this way, both partners can grow comfortable being assertive, while fostering a stable and mutually satisfying relationship.

Determining Self-Confidence Compatibility

Consult the table below and find your Love Vibration in the column corresponding to your gender. Look across to the right column, labeled "Self-Confidence Assessment," and write this rating in your Emotional Interaction Profile or on paper. Repeat this step for your mate or any potential partner.

Male	Female	Self-Confidence Assessment
4, 5, 8, 19, 22	4, 5, 8, 19, 22	Very Secure
2, 3, 6, 7, 14	1, 3, 6, 7, 11	Moderately Secure
1, 9, 11, 16	2, 9, 14, 16	Insecure

Check the next table, labeled "Self-Confidence Compatibility," to identify your assessment for this trait. The rating will either be "Favorable" or "Potentially Difficult." Write this result in your Emotional Interaction Profile.

Review the interpretations following the table. Self-confidence is a crucial personality trait, and it is essential for fostering intimacy. These guidelines can provide insights into your own and your partner's level of self-confidence and how this factor may be impacting your relationship.

Your Assessment	Your Partner	Self-Confidence Compatibility
Very Secure	Very Secure	Potentially Difficult
Very Secure	Moderately Secure	Favorable
Very Secure	Insecure	Potentially Difficult
Moderately Secure	Very Secure	Favorable
Moderately Secure	Moderately Secure	Favorable
Moderately Secure	Insecure	Favorable
Insecure	Very Secure	Potentially Difficult
Insecure	Moderately Secure	Favorable
Insecure	Insecure	Potentially Difficult

Favorable: This assessment portends a stable relationship. Both you and your partner should enjoy a strong bond of personal security and trust. You likely have deep empathy for one another and don't often trigger insecurities. As is true of any intimate relationship, tensions may flare in day-to-day living, but your capacity for mutual understanding and respect, and the strength of your emotional bond, will usually work to minimize disagreements.

Potentially Difficult: With this compatibility assessment, you should be able to maintain a harmonious relationship built on cooperation and mutual respect, assuming you and your partner remain emotionally stable. However, that might be easier said than done, as certain pairings are more prone to friction and discord, as discussed in these next comparisons.

When one partner is insecure: That individual is likely to harbor feelings of mistrust, fear of rejection, and low self-worth. These negative emotions can manifest as jealousy, resentment, and possessiveness. Some insecure mates worry excessively that their partners are cheating or will do so in the future, while others live in constant dread that a breakup is imminent. If these feelings go unchecked, an aura of suspicion, mistrust, and feelings of betrayal may build up and explode like a ruptured pressure cooker, abruptly ending the relationship. Ironically, some insecure people who obsess about a spouse's infidelity resort to the same misconduct, and the fear that a partner might do likewise could be their conscience speaking. Codependency is another distinct possibility that can develop with this pairing.

The best way to sustain the vitality of this relationship requires that the more secure partner make a concerted effort to reassure their mate of their love and devotion. As the saying goes, someone in the room has to be an adult. The potential risk here is that the secure partner may decide that having to be constantly reassuring is too demanding or draining, and they could decide to exit the relationship or let it fall apart on its own. In effect, the insecure mate has caused the very outcome they feared.

Praise, reassurance, and displays of genuine affection can serve as powerful antidotes to such breakdowns and might help some insecure partners grow over time into mature, balanced individuals. An occasional surprise visit or phone call during office hours, and small gifts of sentimental value, can be helpful. Even so, both partners must be invested in the relationship. The insecure partner must also do their part to diligently maintain control of their emotions, guard against jealousy and impulse, and be willing to seek professional help when necessary.

Both partners are insecure: The same guidelines just discussed for a relationship where one partner is insecure apply here, but it is even more crucial that an atmosphere of trust and cooperation be maintained. Both partners should approach their relationship realistically and understand that a minor argument could escalate into a major confrontation that could destroy the relationship. Likewise, both must be willing to work to help one another develop self-confidence and bolster their sense of self-worth. This relationship can only endure if personal growth and maturity are embraced. No future can exist without a foundation of trust, love, and mutual respect.

Determining Extroversion Compatibility

Consult the table below and find your Love Vibration in the column corresponding to your gender. Read across to the third column on the right, labeled "Extroversion Assessment," and write this rating in your Emotional Interaction Profile. Repeat this step for your current mate or any prospective partner.

Male	Female	Extroversion Assessment
1, 3, 5, 14, 19	1, 3, 5, 14, 19	Very Extroverted
4, 8, 11, 16, 22	4, 6, 7, 8, 11	Moderately Extroverted
2, 6, 7, 9	2, 9, 16, 22	Introverted

Refer to the table below, labeled "Extroversion Compatibility," to find your assessment for this trait. Your rating will either be "Favorable" or "Potentially Difficult." Record this evaluation in your Emotional Interaction Profile.

Your Assessment	Your Partner	Extroversion Compatibility
Very Extroverted	Very Extroverted	Potentially Difficult
Very Extroverted	Moderately Extroverted	Favorable
Very Extroverted	Introverted	Potentially Difficult
Moderately Extroverted	Very Extroverted	Favorable
Moderately Extroverted	Moderately Extroverted	Favorable
Moderately Extroverted	Introverted	Favorable
Introverted	Very Extroverted	Potentially Difficult
Introverted	Moderately Extroverted	Favorable
Introverted	Introverted	Potentially Difficult

Review the following interpretations to gain insights into your Extroversion Compatibility assessment and how it could be impacting your relationship.

Favorable: In this harmonious pairing, both partners likely share many common interests and desires. The pace of your social lives and mutual appetite for adventure should align well, permitting you to savor life's joys and challenges together. You may enjoy visiting the same places and taking part in similar activities, creating fertile ground for many cherished memories. While cooperative interaction might not be enough to fully offset potential disparities reflected in other aspects of your numerology chart, it should enhance the vibrancy of your relationship and make conflict resolution easier.

Potentially Difficult: This pairing could be challenging if one partner is significantly more extroverted than the other. The extroverted partner might find the relationship stimulating and enjoyable, while the other individual feels neglected or taken for granted. Feelings of alienation, depression, and jealousy are common among introverted personalities. They may feel excluded from their partner's life, even though it is often by their own choice. Many, if not most, introverts have a strong desire to be needed and appreciated. Companionship and affection are essential to their happiness and well-being.

When conflicts arise in this relationship, the extroverted partner will need to take the initiative and restore equilibrium by, for instance, making an effort to include their introverted mate in social activities. Shared experiences can often have therapeutic value, and an introvert might respond well to such invitations. Absent this proactive gesture, an introverted mate might request or even demand more involvement in their partner's social life. Sometimes, an element of possessiveness might surface. To address this, both partners must discuss their feelings frankly and search for compromise. Otherwise, the introverted partner may pull back emotionally or choose to establish a separate social life, which could put the relationship in jeopardy. Open and honest communication is vital to maintain a healthy and satisfying partnership.

When both partners are introverted: In this relationship, both individuals may feel comfortable with a reserved, quiet lifestyle and desire to spend their time together in intimate settings. However, this pairing can be challenging if their mutual introversion prevents them from occasionally stepping out of their comfort zones. A relationship can become stagnant if both partners avoid new experiences and social interactions. Unhealthy codependencies can also develop.

Two introverts might have different levels of tolerance for solitude and socializing. For instance, one might enjoy an occasional gathering with friends, while the other wishes to avoid such gatherings entirely. Such differences can cause arguments and friction if not effectively managed. To mitigate any potential issues, both partners must know and respect each other's boundaries while also encouraging one another to expand their comfort zones. Open communication about their needs, expectations, and comfort levels is crucial. They should strive for a comfortable balance between nurturing their own need for solitude and enjoying shared experiences, whether it's a quiet evening at home, an occasional night out with friends, or a congenial dinner with family. As long as both partners are considerate of each other's preferences and willing to compromise, this pairing can offer a secure and nurturing environment in which both can flourish.

As we've mentioned before, it is important to remember that when analyzing any interactive personality trait discussed in this chapter, or any aspect of numerology, all relationships require effort, understanding, and mutual respect. No matter what level of Extroversion Compatibility exists between two individuals, with open communication and a willingness to compromise, any relationship can grow and prosper.

Determining Reactivity Compatibility

Consult the table below and locate your Love Vibration in the column corresponding to your gender. Then, read across to the third column, labeled "Reactivity Assessment," and write your rating in your Emotional Interaction Profile or on paper. Do the same for your mate or any potential partner.

ASSESSING YOUR EMOTIONAL INTERACTION | 145

Male	Female	Reactivity Assessment
4, 7, 8, 19, 22	4, 7, 8, 19, 22	Very Stable
2, 3, 6, 9, 16	1, 3, 5, 6, 11	Moderately Stable
1, 5, 11, 14	2, 9, 14, 16	Impulsive

Check the following table, labeled "Reactivity Compatibility," to find your assessment for this trait. The rating will be either "Favorable" or "Potentially Difficult." Record this result in your Emotional Interaction Profile.

Your Assessment	Your Partner	Reactivity Compatibility
Very Stable	Very Stable	Favorable
Very Stable	Moderately Stable	Favorable
Very Stable	Impulsive	Potentially Difficult
Moderately Stable	Very Stable	Favorable
Moderately Stable	Moderately Stable	Favorable
Moderately Stable	Impulsive	Potentially Difficult
Impulsive	Very Stable	Potentially Difficult
Impulsive	Moderately Stable	Potentially Difficult
Impulsive	Impulsive	Potentially Difficult

Review the interpretations below for insights into how your Reactivity Compatibility assessment might be impacting your relationship dynamics.

Favorable: Stability is the bedrock upon which vibrant and enduring romantic partnerships are built. When two partners share this quality, it can greatly enhance their prospects for enduring intimacy. In this pairing, your mutual dispositions harmonize, and you both approach life with pragmatism and purpose. You understand each other's temperaments, and this allows you both to navigate the nuances of daily life with grace and empathy. Your mutual stability lays a firm foundation for deep intimacy. By acting as a stabilizing presence for each other, you can alleviate potential conflicts and focus on building a vibrant romance. Cooperative interaction will not only provide a buffer against potential issues that may exist in other aspects of your numerology chart but will also amplify the resilience and longevity of your relationship. Ultimately, two stable partners can set the stage for a lasting bond that weathers life's storms while still basking in its gentle breezes.

Potentially Difficult: A mismatch in the Stability aspect can disrupt relationship equilibrium and introduce significant imbalances. When one partner is steadfast and composed, and the other is prone to impulsivity, the resulting dynamics can test their will to remain involved. The unpredictable behavior of an impulsive partner, their mood swings, possessiveness, and flares of jealousy, can take a heavy emotional toll on the stable partner. When the stable mate bears the responsibility of maintaining calm and balance, it can be emotionally draining over time. It's crucial to navigate these dynamics mindfully to safeguard the relationship's durability.

Both partners are impulsive: Relationships of this kind can be intense, even volatile, and while this spontaneity may spark excitement, it could also lead to a short-lived romance that ends with memorable fireworks. Without a stabilizing influence, tension and hostility can erupt, exacerbated by impulsivity and volatile moods. To salvage such a relationship, both partners must commit to building a calm, stable environment. They must control their moods and avoid arguing or engaging in provocative actions that may escalate into major conflicts. The urge to escape into illicit affairs must be resisted, as reckless flings are almost always discovered and may destroy mutual trust. With cooperation, self-discipline, and willpower, there is hope that even the most tumultuous love affair can be transformed into a fulfilling and long-lasting relationship.

One partner is very stable, and the other is impulsive: In this dynamic, tension will be present from the start. Unless the stable partner is willing to continually foster equilibrium, the connection may unravel quickly. The stable partner, who typically seeks a balanced, harmonious love life, may struggle with the unpredictability of an impulsive mate. The resulting frustration may tempt the former to respond negatively to provocations, making matters worse, or they might simply walk away. Preventing a cycle of discord and mutual self-destruction requires tolerance and empathy from the stable partner and self-control and stability from the impulsive one.

One partner is moderately stable, the other is impulsive: Similar pitfalls exist in this scenario, but a moderately stable person might have a better understanding of their impulsive partner's feelings and reactions. This understanding can pave the way for better communication and interaction, helping to minimize potential damage and create a roadmap for mutual growth and relationship strengthening.

Determining Agreeableness Compatibility

Consult the table below and locate your Love Vibration in the column corresponding to your gender. Then, read across to the third column, labeled "Agreeableness Assessment," and write down your rating in your Emotional Interaction Profile or on paper. Do the same for your mate or any prospective partner.

Male	Female	Agreeableness Assessment
2, 6, 9, 11, 19	2, 6, 9, 11, 19	Very Cooperative
1, 3, 4, 5, 7	3, 5, 7, 16, 22	Moderately Cooperative
8, 14, 16, 22	1, 4, 8, 14	Stubborn

Refer to the next table, labeled "Agreeableness Compatibility," to find your assessment. The rating will be "Favorable" or "Potentially Difficult." Write it down in your Emotional Interaction Profile. Then, review the interpretations that follow to gain insights into how your Agreeableness Compatibility assessment may be impacting your relationship dynamics.

Your Assessment	Your Partner	Agreeableness Compatibility
Very Cooperative	Very Cooperative	Favorable
Very Cooperative	Moderately Cooperative	Favorable
Very Cooperative	Stubborn	Potentially Difficult
Moderately Cooperative	Very Cooperative	Favorable
Moderately Cooperative	Moderately Cooperative	Favorable
Moderately Cooperative	Stubborn	Favorable
Stubborn	Very Cooperative	Potentially Difficult
Stubborn	Moderately Cooperative	Favorable
Stubborn	Stubborn	Potentially Difficult

Favorable: A relationship cannot endure, let alone flourish, without ongoing cooperation between partners. When their Agreeableness assessment is compatible, it can lend immense depth and durability to a romance. Rather than perpetually wrestling with their differences, partners can focus on cherishing the qualities they admire in each other and build a deeply satisfying, potentially lifelong bond. A "Favorable" rating here indicates a willingness to share the responsibilities of deep intimacy and support each other's growth. As problems arise in daily life, you should be able to easily overcome them and make meaningful improvements to your relationship without encountering stubborn resistance. Your mutual ability to compromise will help avert misunderstandings and discord. Provided you and your partner maintain this optimal level of cooperation, you can look forward to enjoying a progressive and mutually rewarding romance for years to come.

Potentially Difficult: Partners who are highly devoted to one another should be able to work out any differences that arise in daily life, maintaining cooperative and harmonious interaction. However, those who are stubborn may benefit from the suggestions offered below.

One partner is very cooperative, the other is stubborn: Numerous problems may crop up in this relationship. Tension can build as the cooperative partner continuously yields to the other's will. If the more agreeable partner feels consigned to a submissive role or believes that their desires and feelings are being overlooked, they may begin to exhibit stubbornness or animosity, which could undermine the relationship. A lack of give-and-take will lead, sooner or later, to discord and erosion of mutual respect. If this relationship is to endure, the stubborn partner must develop both flexibility and sensitivity, while adopting a more cooperative approach and a willingness to consider their partner's perspectives and needs, both in romance and daily life.

One partner is moderately cooperative, and the other is stubborn: The potential pitfalls in this relationship are similar to those discussed in the previous assessment but to a lesser extent. Moderately cooperative partners will each have stubborn streaks and be more inclined to stand their ground, demanding that their wants and needs be met. This will invariably incite loud arguments and hurt feelings from time to time, but neither partner is likely to become submissive or develop animosity over being taken for granted. Simply put, they will be better able to handle the other's stubborn streak.

Both partners are stubborn: Relationships in this category are often strained by a generalized lack of cooperation and arguments fueled by stubborn obstinacy. Resentment could develop as a consequence. Neither partner may be willing to budge from their demands or views, leading to a stand-off. Both may hold out for short-term wins in getting their way, despite the negative impact such stubbornness may have on their relationship. Compromises based on give-and-take may be few and far between.

Ironically, this lack of compatibility may not necessarily spell doom for the relationship. Stubborn partners sometimes remain together for years in a dysfunctional relationship built on simmering resentment because neither is willing to change or admit that their connection has failed. Friends and onlookers might whisper that these unhappy souls stay together for no other reason than to make each other miserable.

To restore peace and harmony to such a relationship, both individuals must learn to yield and compromise. Successful relationships are built on a foundation of cooperation and mutual trust. If both partners commit to improving their communication and developing a more versatile partnership where both can have their way without it being at the other's expense, hope burns eternal that even the most dysfunctional relationship can be revitalized.

A Final Thought

When you've calculated all five aspects of the Emotional Interaction chart, as described in this chapter, and reviewed the interpretations, you should possess a wealth of valuable insights into your romantic relationships. Bear in mind that the assessments presented in these pages reflect typical responses and behavior within intimate relationships. For instance, "very assertive" implies that you usually assume the initiative, but not always, and sometimes in less evident ways. Similarly, "passive" does not mean that a partner is always docile or compliant. A passive individual at times might exhibit assertiveness, such as passive-aggressive behavior.

The qualities assigned to each numerological vibration are accurate, but life experiences and day-to-day interactions in a relationship can alter a person's core attitudes and reactions. Numerology provides signposts indicating how the spectrum of vibrations can influence us if we don't take conscious action to modify their impact. Ultimately, humans are born with free will, which means we can learn, change, and grow. This evolution isn't always reflected in a numerology chart.

Interactive Analysis can be a valuable tool for analyzing the emotional compatibility of any two individuals in a romantic context. It can reveal attitudes, desires, habits, and behaviors, providing a glimpse into how we interact with others. Use these techniques to ensure that your love life is rich and satisfying, and your romantic relationships are stable and enduring as you move forward in your journey through life.

Chapter 10
Assessing Your Sexual Interaction

*I*n this chapter, we will shift our focus from analyzing emotional interaction to sexual compatibility. We will explore how numerology, and specifically the tools of Interactive Analysis, can help partners who are disillusioned with physical intimacy or face challenges threatening the stability of their relationships. And we'll answer an important question: When two people are truly committed to building a mutually satisfying partnership, and if given the tools and insights necessary to effect meaningful change, is it possible for them to improve and deepen their physical bond?

Sexual fulfillment is a significant concern for many people in everyday existence. Some are seeking new intimacy, while others are already involved in relationships marred by sexual dysfunction. They watch their romances deteriorating but lack solutions to identify what is broken, much less fix it. And even if they had such tools and insights, not every romance can be salvaged. When sexual attraction fades, it becomes increasingly difficult to resuscitate, and turmoil soon clouds every aspect of the relationship, forcing partners to walk away.

Fortunately, it is possible for individuals to proactively take steps to prevent or repair dysfunction in physical intimacy. Perhaps there's dissonance in your temperaments—where you are demonstrative and uninhibited, while your mate is reserved and less affectionate. Maybe you each have different likes or dislikes in bed. You might both seek to be the dominant partner, or insecurities detract from your pleasure. Using numerology to identify such incompatibilities and sources of discord in a sexual partnership can help you address those issues before they snowball into crises beyond repair. This approach can help you work through differences, enhance physical interaction and compatibility, and strengthen the durability of your connection. Using numerology to inject positive change into your intimacy can pave the way to a brighter future of physical gratification and romantic bliss. This chapter will serve as a guide on that journey.

Numerologists recognize that some partners are naturally attuned and more compatible than others. They can pinpoint clear reasons why this is so in the partners' numerology charts. By analyzing complementary and conflicting vibrations that play a major role in sexual interaction, we can deduce whether a relationship will thrive, and what should be done to address a clash of opposing personalities and desires that could erupt into discord and chaos.

As discussed in Chapter 9, numerology offers a precise and accurate method, Interactive Analysis, to reveal insights into the compatibility between two individuals. Previously, we analyzed five key personality traits in the Emotional Interaction Profile. Now, we will move on to explore the Sexual Interaction Profile, which similarly focuses on a set of five traits that can significantly impact physical intimacy. The techniques outlined here utilize the same tools described previously but focus on using Interactive Analysis to enhance sexual compatibility. These methods can identify potential sources of sexual discord and reduce tension, offering a path to rehabilitate even the most dysfunctional relationships marred by sexual incompatibility, conflicting personalities, or infidelity.

A sample Sexual Interaction Profile chart appears on the next page. Blank templates are provided at the end of this book. You can jot down your numerological calculations on these pages or make photocopies before you begin working through these steps. Alternatively, you can use notebook paper to record your calculations and compatibility assessments. Either way, writing down your chart calculation allows you to conveniently compare various aspects of the chart and provides a record of your results so you don't have to repeat all of these steps again.

Sexual Interaction Profile

Behavioral Compatibility (Dominant/Passive)		
You	Your Partner	Assessment

Self-Confidence Compatibility (Uninhibited/Inhibited)		
You	Your Partner	Assessment

Physicality Compatibility (Demonstrative/Reserved)		
You	Your Partner	Assessment

Reactivity Compatibility (Spontaneous/Controlled)		
You	Your Partner	Assessment

Agreeableness Compatibility (Openminded/Conventional)		
You	Your Partner	Assessment

For the methods discussed in this chapter, you must know the Sexual Consensus vibration for yourself and your partner. If you have not yet completed your basic numerology chart, refer to Chapter 2 and follow the instructions provided for Step #3. Once you have determined both Sexual Consensus vibrations, you can proceed with evaluating your sexual compatibility.

Determining Behavioral Compatibility

In the table below, locate your Sexual Consensus vibration in the column corresponding to your gender. Read across to the right column, labeled "Behavioral Assessment," to find your evaluation. The options are "Dominant," "Heterogeneous," and "Passive." Heterogeneous refers to a personality type that includes both dominant and passive traits, suggesting a balanced or more nuanced approach that falls somewhere between Dominant and Passive. Repeat this step for your mate.

Male	Female	Behavioral Assessment
1, 5, 8, 14, 19	1, 5, 8, 14, 16	Dominant
3, 7, 11, 16, 22	3, 6, 11, 19, 22	Heterogeneous
2, 4, 6, 9	2, 4, 7, 9	Passive

Check the table below, labeled "Behavioral Compatibility," for an assessment of your interaction with your partner. The rating will be either "Favorable" or "Potentially Difficult." Write this result in your Sexual Interaction Profile, and then review the interpretations given in the following pages to understand how your Behavioral compatibility may impact the dynamics of your sexual relationship.

Your Assessment	Your Partner	Behavioral Compatibility
Dominant	Dominant	Potentially Difficult
Dominant	Heterogeneous	Favorable
Dominant	Passive	Potentially Difficult
Heterogeneous	Dominant	Favorable
Heterogeneous	Heterogeneous	Favorable
Heterogeneous	Passive	Favorable
Passive	Dominant	Potentially Difficult
Passive	Heterogeneous	Favorable
Passive	Passive	Potentially Difficult

Favorable: If this assessment applies to your relationship, it reflects a high degree of sexual compatibility in the realm of your day-to-day behavior. You and your partner know how to share control without competing or seeking to impose your desires on each other. You understand when to compromise, and you can do so without causing stress or misunderstandings. This positive interaction promotes deep, lasting satisfaction, provided both partners use common sense in managing their physical relationship. Here are a few further insights on specific pairings:

Two heterogeneous partners: When both partners have a mix of dominant and passive traits, they can create a balanced dynamic in their physical intimacy. They will understand each other's needs for both control and surrender, which lays the foundation for harmonious interaction. This compatibility assessment is very favorable.

Heterogeneous partner with a dominant or passive partner: Typically compatible. The heterogeneous partner's ability to adapt and balance their mix of dominant and passive behaviors can complement a partner who leans toward either dominance or passivity. This pairing can create a dynamic that is exciting and rewarding for both partners. However, open and honest communication, and mutual respect, are crucial to maintaining a healthy, stable relationship. By embracing their diversity of traits and finding a balance between dominance and passivity, these partners can establish fulfilling and enduring sexual compatibility.

Potentially Difficult: With this assessment, you and your partner should be able to work out your differences while maintaining stable interaction. However, many individuals find it challenging to make the adjustments necessary to ensure a satisfying relationship. Understanding the common pitfalls and remedies associated with your particular behavioral pairing can be highly beneficial.

Two dominant partners: Frequent arguments and a lack of cooperation are common pitfalls in this pairing. Both partners may struggle to maintain dominance, imposing their likes and dislikes on each other, provoking anger and discord. Both must learn to control their dominating instincts, be willing to compromise, and focus on areas of compatibility and shared interests to maintain harmony. If one partner resists positive change, the other should take the initiative by avoiding conflict and assuming a more adaptable role. If stubbornness persists, re-evaluating the viability of the relationship may be necessary.

One partner is dominant, and the other is passive: At first glance, this would appear to be a compatible pairing. However, in these relationships, the passive partner will often feel bullied, abused, or taken for granted. This can result in hypersensitivity, depression, and lowered confidence, as well as the danger of the relationship becoming abusive. An individual who believes they are in an abusive sexual relationship should seek professional counseling or terminate the affair before matters escalate. In other cases, restoring or strengthening harmonious interaction will require the dominant partner to develop self-control and patience, while the passive partner must stand up for themselves and accept new responsibilities as an equal. If the stronger partner refuses to make improvements, a candid discussion might be necessary. If no positive change occurs, the viability of the relationship should be reconsidered.

Two passive partners: Confusion, instability, and conflict can throw these relationships off balance. Passive individuals typically lack assertiveness and expect their partner to take the lead, but when neither is willing to do so, the relationship can become vulnerable to confusion or stagnation. Both partners need to recognize this potential pitfall and take turns being assertive to create a stable and mutually satisfying relationship.

These assessments offer insights into how your Behavioral interaction can either enhance or undermine physical intimacy. By understanding and addressing potential challenges, you can undertake significant improvements in a relationship and build the foundation for greater pleasure and a happier future.

Assessing Self-Confidence Compatibility

Consult the table below and locate your Sexual Consensus vibration in the column corresponding to your gender. Check the third column, labeled "Self-Confidence Assessment," for your rating and record this in your Sexual Interaction Profile. The ratings are "Uninhibited/Secure," "Heterogeneous," and "Inhibited/ Insecure." Do the same for your partner.

Male	Female	Self-Confidence Assessment
1, 3, 5, 8, 22	1, 3, 5, 8, 22	Uninhibited/Secure
6, 11, 14, 19	6, 11, 14, 19	Heterogeneous
2, 4, 7, 9, 16	2, 4, 7, 9, 16	Inhibited/Insecure

Refer to the following table, labeled "Self-Confidence Compatibility," to deduce your assessment for this trait. The rating will be "Favorable" or "Potentially Difficult." Enter this result in your Sexual Interaction Profile, and then review the interpretations that follow to learn how this factor could be impacting the dynamics of your sexual relationship.

Your Assessment	Your Partner	Self-Confidence Compatibility
Uninhibited/Secure	Uninhibited/Secure	Potentially Difficult
Uninhibited/Secure	Heterogeneous	Favorable
Uninhibited/Secure	Inhibited/Insecure	Potentially Difficult
Heterogeneous	Uninhibited/Secure	Favorable
Heterogeneous	Heterogeneous	Favorable
Heterogeneous	Inhibited/Insecure	Favorable
Inhibited/Insecure	Uninhibited/Secure	Potentially Difficult
Inhibited/Insecure	Heterogeneous	Favorable
Inhibited/Insecure	Inhibited/Insecure	Potentially Difficult

Favorable: This pairing usually produces a stable sexual relationship where you and your partner enjoy a strong sense of personal security and mutual respect. You have empathy for one another and don't usually trigger insecurities. As with any intimate relationship, everyday disagreements can cause upsets and tempers to flare, but your capacity for mutual trust and understanding should neutralize any disruptive fallout. This positive Self-Confidence interaction can work to improve sexual fulfillment, with you both feeling empowered to openly express yourselves and enjoy your lives together.

Additional insights on specific pairings follow.

Both partners are heterogeneous: If both partners have a mix of inhibited and uninhibited tendencies, they can establish a dynamic and richly rewarding sexual connection. This pairing fosters growth as the partners navigate their feelings and learn to overcome their insecurities together. By supporting and uplifting one another, they can contribute to each other's sense of self-worth and confidence. However, open communication and empathy must be maintained in this relationship. Through cooperation and reassurance, they can achieve a resilient sexual bond and share an exciting adventure of self-discovery.

Heterogeneous partner and an uninhibited partner: This pairing favors a sexual connection that is exciting, resilient, and fun. The uninhibited partner will encourage their heterogeneous mate to explore new ideas and activities that can lead to mutual pleasure. However, the heterogeneous partner's boundaries must be respected, and this must be done in a way that does not trigger their insecurities, causing them to become more inhibited rather than less so. By fostering an atmosphere of mutual trust and nurturing a spirit of adventure in this relationship, both partners can look forward to a progressive and enjoyable sexual relationship.

Heterogeneous partner and an inhibited partner: While compatible, these individuals may find it necessary to invest considerable patience in the physical side of their relationship. The heterogeneous partner's often unpredictable mix of uninhibited and restrained behaviors will never be boring. Both partners must work to build a mutually supportive environment that will encourage the inhibited mate to grow beyond their insecurities and not fear open, honest communication. The heterogeneous partner can facilitate this by being patient and supportive, allowing their mate to work through their inhibitions at their own pace. Over time, this relationship can grow strong and vibrant, providing a framework for mutual satisfaction and enjoyment.

Potentially Difficult: While it might be challenging at times, you should be able to build a mutually satisfying physical relationship, provided that both you and your partner maintain emotional stability. Disagreements or uncomfortable moments involving inhibitions or generalized feelings of insecurity may develop at times, especially when one partner has suffered violent or abusive sexual trauma in a previous relationship.

One partner is inhibited: The inhibited partner is likely to harbor feelings of mistrust or fear of rejection. They might also doubt their physical appeal or prowess in bed, or grapple with a general feeling of low self-esteem. If not addressed, these negative emotions may grow into jealous and possessive behavior. Insecure individuals often worry incessantly that their partners are, or may soon be, cheating on them. They may also live with the constant fear that a breakup is imminent. This can lead to a partner's innocent actions being misconstrued and cause the insecure mate to erupt in anger over a harmless smile or greeting. The resulting tension and discord may cause a relationship to crumble into a web of accusations and hurt feelings. Ironically, some insecure people who obsess about a partner's infidelity may be indulging in the same unfaithful behavior themselves. Unhealthy codependency is another possibility with this pairing.

The best chance of sustaining a relationship where one person is inhibited and the other is not will require the latter to make an ongoing effort to offer frequent reassurance of their love and devotion. One downside to this is that the secure individual may eventually decide that this constant outpouring is too emotionally draining, causing them to pull away from intimacy or eventually terminate the relationship. In effect, the insecure person has caused the outcome they feared most.

Praise, reassurance, and frequent displays of affection can be potent antidotes to this destructive cycle and may help some inhibited partners grow into mature, balanced individuals. Occasional gestures, such as surprise visits or calls during office hours, and small gifts of sentimental value, are particularly helpful. Still, it takes two to keep a relationship vibrant, and an inhibited partner must make an ongoing effort to reciprocate by working to control their emotions, guarding against jealousy and self-doubt, and seeking professional help when necessary.

Both partners are inhibited: The guidelines for a relationship with one inhibited partner just discussed apply here as well. However, it is even more crucial that an element of cooperation and trust be nurtured. Both partners should approach their sexual intimacy with realistic expectations and understand that a minor disagreement could escalate into a major argument and end the relationship at a moment's notice. Both must diligently strive to help each other cultivate self-confidence and strengthen their self-image and confidence. This relationship can thrive only if both partners take the initiative to grow and mature, as individuals and as a team. Building a future on trust, love, and mutual respect is crucial.

Assessing Physicality Compatibility

Locate your Sexual Consensus vibration in the table below, and then read across to the "Physicality Assessment" column to find your compatibility rating. The ratings are "Demonstrative," "Heterogeneous," and "Reserved." Enter this rating in your

Sexual Interaction Profile, and then repeat this step for your mate or any prospective partner.

Male	Female	Physicality Assessment
1, 3, 5, 8, 14	1, 5, 8, 11, 16, 22	Demonstrative
6, 11, 16, 19, 22	3, 6, 14, 19	Heterogeneous
2, 4, 7, 9	2, 4, 7, 9	Reserved

Consult the table below to determine your assessment, and note it in your Sexual Interaction Profile. The rating will be either "Favorable" or "Potentially Difficult."

Your Assessment	Your Partner	Physicality Compatibility
Demonstrative	Demonstrative	Potentially Difficult
Demonstrative	Heterogeneous	Favorable
Demonstrative	Reserved	Potentially Difficult
Heterogeneous	Demonstrative	Favorable
Heterogeneous	Heterogeneous	Favorable
Heterogeneous	Reserved	Favorable
Reserved	Demonstrative	Potentially Difficult
Reserved	Heterogeneous	Favorable
Reserved	Reserved	Potentially Difficult

Review the following interpretations for insights into your Physicality Compatibility assessment and how this dynamic could be impacting your sexual relationship.

Favorable: In this harmonious pairing, both partners likely share many common interests and desires in the realm of sexual intimacy. They understand each other well, and their physical needs and preferences probably align. They are willing to fulfill one another's desires and truly enjoy their time together. Compatibility in the Physicality aspect of a numerology chart typically enhances both individuals' sense of overall satisfaction in their sexual relationship and establishes the foundation for deeply pleasurable intimacy.

Both partners are heterogeneous: When both individuals exhibit a blend of demonstrative and reserved behaviors, they infuse an unusual but intriguing mix of sexuality into their physical relationship. This pairing can create a unique dynamic where each partner has the opportunity to explore and appreciate the deeper aspects of their physicality. This nuanced interaction can bring passion, excitement, and an uninhibited openness into the relationship, as well as depth and a hint of mystery. Both individuals will have opportunities to learn from and inspire each other. The interplay between them can open the door to a rich and intensely satisfying exploration of physical intimacy. By embracing their diverse personalities and seeking a balance between demonstrativeness and restraint, these partners can achieve a rare and deeply satisfying level of intimacy in their romance.

One partner is heterogeneous, the other is demonstrative: This pairing blends the dynamic energy of a demonstrative partner with the more nuanced traits of a heterogeneous mate who alternates between affectionate and reserved. The former can bring passion and spontaneity into the relationship, fueling a sense of adventure. The latter contributes an unpredictability that will keep intimacy fresh and interesting while infusing an element of restraint to temper their mate's intensity.

In this pairing, the heterogeneous partner's ability to adapt and balance their behaviors plays a vital role. They complement the demonstrative partner's enthusiasm by creating a sense of security and encouraging a deeper intimate connection. However, the demonstrative partner must respect their mate's boundaries and not allow their passion to overwhelm or push them beyond their comfort zone. Open communication, empathy, and mutual respect are key to maintaining a healthy sexual relationship. Both partners must actively listen to each other's desires and concerns. By embracing the diversity of their physicality and finding a harmonious balance between the contrasting aspects of their personalities, this pairing can create a sexual connection that is both exciting and nurturing.

One partner is heterogeneous, and the other is reserved: This pairing unites the contrasting traits of a heterogeneous partner with a more restrained partner, creating a sexual connection that blends depth, mystery, and restraint. The heterogeneous mate's ability to adapt and balance their behaviors can create a favorable environment for the reserved partner to explore their desires and overcome their inhibitions. In this relationship, the reserved partner may feel a sense of safety and security with their heterogeneous mate. However, the more affectionate partner must be attentive to their lover's needs, allowing them to open up at their own pace and respecting their boundaries. Honest communication and empathy are crucial to the success of this sexual connection. Both partners must be willing to openly share their desires, fears, and boundaries to create a comfortable and mutually supportive environment. By embracing the diversity of their physicality and nurturing a sense of trust, these partners can build a vibrant and fulfilling sexual relationship.

Potentially Difficult: When one partner is more physically affectionate and demonstrative than the other, a relationship may be challenging. The more demonstrative partner may find the sexual connection stimulating and enjoyable, while the reserved partner may feel overwhelmed or that their personal space is being violated. Feelings of alienation and depression are common reactions in reserved personalities who worry that they cannot respond as ardently, or they aren't capable of satisfying their partner's needs. Many reserved individuals have a strong desire for affection and connection. When this is the case, their happiness depends on being able to enjoy physical intimacy in a way that aligns with their comfort level.

When misunderstandings arise in this relationship, the demonstrative partner must take the initiative and restore equilibrium. This can be done by showing sensitivity to their mate's needs and preferences, which helps to ensure that sex is mutually enjoyable rather than intimidating or overwhelming. Finding a balance between intensity and restraint can create an environment where both partners feel valued and fulfilled in their physical connection.

Both partners are reserved: In this relationship, both individuals may prefer a quiet and discreet approach to intimacy. They may share similar preferences for spending time in intimate settings and enjoying each other's companionship. However, they must ensure that this quiet lifestyle doesn't impede their expression of affection or limit sexual interaction. A relationship can become stagnant if both partners refrain from physical affection or avoid stepping out of their comfort zones. It's also crucial to remember that two reserved partners may have different responses to affection, sexual interaction, and experimentation. Recognizing and managing these differences is crucial to maintaining a healthy balance in the relationship.

To mitigate potential issues, both partners must respect one another's boundaries while at the same time encouraging open communication about sexual needs and expectations. Finding a balance between their competing needs and desires will allow them to develop a nurturing relationship in which both can flourish and enjoy one another.

Determining Reactivity Compatibility

Refer to the following table and find your Sexual Consensus vibration in the column corresponding to your gender. Read across to the third column, labeled "Reactivity Assessment," to determine your rating. Enter it in your Sexual Interaction Profile. The possible ratings are "Spontaneous," "Heterogeneous," and "Controlled." Do the same for your mate or potential partner.

Male	Female	Reactivity Assessment
1, 3, 5, 14, 19	1, 3, 5, 11, 19	Spontaneous
2, 6, 11, 16	2, 6, 7, 14, 16	Heterogeneous
4, 8, 7, 9, 22	4, 8, 9, 22	Controlled

Refer to this next table, labeled "Reactivity Compatibility," to find your assessment for this trait. The rating will be either "Favorable" or "Potentially Difficult." Record the result in your Sexual Interaction Profile.

Your Assessment	Your Partner	Reactivity Compatibility
Spontaneous	Spontaneous	Favorable
Spontaneous	Heterogeneous	Favorable
Spontaneous	Controlled	Potentially Difficult
Heterogeneous	Spontaneous	Favorable
Heterogeneous	Heterogeneous	Favorable
Heterogeneous	Controlled	Potentially Difficult
Controlled	Spontaneous	Potentially Difficult
Controlled	Heterogeneous	Potentially Difficult
Controlled	Controlled	Potentially Difficult

Review these interpretations to learn how your Reactivity Compatibility assessment could be impacting your relationship.

Favorable: When the Reactivity Assessment is compatible, the potential to achieve deep physical intimacy is significantly enhanced. Each partner understands the other's temperament and can bring spontaneity, curiosity, and a sense of adventure into the relationship. Working together, they can forge a connection built on openness, honesty, and acceptance, encouraging one another to try new experiences and explore their desires and fantasies. Further insights for specific pairings are provided below.

One partner is heterogeneous, the other is spontaneous: This combination favors a delightful interplay of distinct energies and styles reflecting each partner's individuality. The spontaneous partner's embrace of newness and adventure can inject excitement into the relationship, while the heterogeneous mate's somewhat more grounded disposition and ability to switch responses can introduce an element of unpredictability that will keep the relationship fresh and their mate intrigued. With this pairing, a dynamic sexual relationship could evolve, permitting both partners to explore their deeper desires and fantasies while building a foundation of trust and empathy. Each must respect the other's boundaries and strike a balance between spontaneity and a grounded approach to intimacy.

Both partners are spontaneous: This pairing can lead to an intense and potentially volatile relationship, sparking initial excitement but often producing a short-lived romance that ends on a sour note. Without a stabilizing influence, both partners are rudderless and may yield to impulsive desires, potentially triggering conflicts and discord that could erode the emotional portion of the relationship. To maintain stability, both partners must moderate their spontaneity and strive for compromise. Taking turns, with one partner being spontaneous and the other keeping their feet on the ground, is the best way to keep this relationship vibrant. Another potential pitfall here is that impulsiveness in bed could cause one partner or the other to feel hurt or rejected. The urge to pursue illicit affairs must be curtailed, as an impulsive fling could irreparably erode mutual trust. However, with cooperation, balance, and self-control, even the most unpredictable and tumultuous love affair has the potential to evolve into a satisfying relationship.

Both partners are heterogeneous: In this pairing, both partners can switch to different roles and behaviors, creating an intimate connection that remains flexible and never becomes stale. Both can easily adapt to the other's needs and desires, fostering understanding and encouraging mutual exploration.

The interplay between their spontaneous and controlled traits can forge a unique and potentially intense sexual relationship, with each partner taking turns leading and following, sharing their desires, and accommodating the other's needs. Candid communication about their desires and boundaries is vital to maintain harmony. By embracing their shared diversity and flexibility, these partners can build a rich and evolving bond.

Potentially Difficult: A Reactivity mismatch can produce significant challenges and imbalances in physical intimacy. If one partner is spontaneous in bed and the other is controlled, tensions will almost certainly simmer. The spontaneous mate's impulsive, unpredictable nature will clash with the measured, deliberate approach of the controlled partner. The former may seek novelty and excitement, while the latter seeks stability and security. These contrasting motivations could trigger frequent misunderstandings and introduce significant emotional strain in the relationship. Both partners must be willing to hear and appreciate one another's perspectives and negotiate a balance that embraces a blend of spontaneity and stability in physical intimacy.

One partner is spontaneous, the other is controlled: With this pairing, an aura of tension and discord may be palpable from the start. The spontaneous partner's desire for excitement and adventure will clash with the down-to-earth mate's need for stability and security. It would be like forcing one individual intent on a one-stand stand into a relationship with someone who yearns for a happy marriage, children, and family. Unless they find a middle ground for compromise, this relationship will have little chance of success. To maintain equilibrium, both partners must recognize and respect each other's contrasting desires. The down-to-earth mate can offer support and dependability, while the spontaneous mate can bring passion and excitement, but both influences must be modulated. This could establish a balance allowing the relationship to evolve into one that both would find satisfying. Open communication, compromise, and a willingness to embrace each other's contrasting desires and dispositions are crucial to the stability and longevity of this relationship.

One partner is heterogeneous, and the other is controlled: In this pairing, the interplay between the partners can create an intriguing foundation for mutual gratification. The down-to-earth partner's practical and grounded approach offers stability and security, while the heterogeneous mate adds spontaneity and adaptability. Out of these seemingly contrasting qualities, there could be fertile ground for a unique blend of stability, security, intimacy, and excitement to take root. Mutual respect and honest communication are crucial to keep this relationship vibrant and to ensure that both partners are satisfied without being pushed beyond their comfort zone.

Assessing Agreeableness Compatibility

Consult the table below and locate your Sexual Consensus vibration in the column corresponding to your gender. Read across to the right column, labeled "Agreeableness Assessment" to find your evaluation. The rating options are: "Open-minded," "Heterogeneous," and "Conventional." Note this in your Sexual Interaction Profile.

Repeat this procedure for your mate or any potential partner.

Male	Female	Agreeableness Assessment
1, 3, 5, 11, 19	1, 3, 5, 6, 19	Open-minded
2, 6, 7, 14, 16	2, 7, 11, 14, 16	Heterogeneous
4, 8, 9, 22	4, 8, 9, 22	Conventional

Refer to this next table, labeled "Agreeableness Compatibility," to find your evaluation for this particular aspect. The options will be either "Favorable" or "Potentially Difficult." Note this result in your Sexual Interaction Profile.

Your Assessment	Your Partner	Agreeableness Compatibility
Open-minded	Open-minded	Favorable
Open-minded	Heterogeneous	Favorable
Open-minded	Conventional	Potentially Difficult
Heterogeneous	Open-minded	Favorable
Heterogeneous	Heterogeneous	Favorable
Heterogeneous	Conventional	Potentially Difficult
Conventional	Open-minded	Potentially Difficult
Conventional	Heterogeneous	Potentially Difficult
Conventional	Conventional	Potentially Difficult

Review the following interpretations to discover how your Agreeableness Compatibility assessment could be impacting the dynamics of your sexual relationship.

Favorable: Agreeableness compatibility can significantly enhance sexual enjoyment and satisfaction, so this evaluation is ideal. Generally, any combination of open-minded and heterogeneous partners will be compatible with one another, but here are some observations on specific pairings.

Both partners are open-minded: Highly compatible, these lovers are capable of forging an exciting and passionate sexual relationship. Both will be open to new experiences, exploring fantasies, and pushing boundaries. Each brings passion, curiosity, and a sense of adventure into the mix. They embrace honest communication and will encourage one another to share their deepest feelings. They enjoy listening to spicy confessions, asking blunt questions, and discussing their own needs and desires. With this congenial, nonjudgmental interaction, deep rapport and trust can develop very quickly. To maintain the vibrancy of this relationship, open communication and honesty are essential and will enable these partners to evolve together in a unique and wonderful journey to intimacy.

Both partners are heterogeneous: Also highly compatible, these partners will be cooperative, adaptable, and capable of deep intimacy. They share a mix of progressive and traditional, which can meld excitement and stability into their relationship. They may think of one another not only as lovers but BFFs (best friends forever). Free-spirited, inquisitive, and fun-loving, some of their sexual interests may border on the provocative. However, both partners have a grounded, practical side that will help to ensure their relationship stays on track and does not veer off into extremes. By embracing their similarities and differences, they will be able to achieve a pleasurable and evolving partnership.

One partner is open-minded; the other is heterogeneous: This combination can bring together an intriguing blend of perspectives and experiences. The open-minded partner offers spontaneity, adventure, and a desire to explore new boundaries, while the heterogeneous mate provides stability and down-to-earth perspectives, but with a dash of fun-loving spirit thrown in. The key to making this relationship work is finding a balance between adventure and stability. Familiarity, which develops over time, and honest communication, will enable these partners to know and respect one another's needs, desires, and boundaries, ensuring that both feel respected and fulfilled. By embracing each other's unique perspectives and finding a middle ground, they will be able to build a sexual connection that is vibrant, satisfying, and anchored in shared values.

Potentially Difficult: In relationships where a mismatch in Agreeableness exists, the partners' personalities and views will not be in sync. Challenges and conflicts may arise, and how these differences might play out depends on the specific pairing, as discussed in the following passages.

One partner is open-minded, the other is conventional: Disagreements can flare in this relationship due to the partners' contrasting attitudes. Resentment, or even hostility, might bubble up when the open-minded partner must continually yield to the conventional mate's stubborn will and comes to believe that their own needs and desires don't matter. The level of cooperation in this pairing is typically low, and this can fuel quarrels, generate discord, and erode mutual respect. For this relationship to survive, the conventional partner must develop empathy and adopt a flexible, cooperative approach to their partner's needs and desires. Open communication is vital, and compromise will help to establish a framework in which these individuals can learn to interact in healthy ways and revitalize their intimacy.

One partner is heterogeneous, the other is conventional: The pitfalls inherent in this relationship are the same as those mentioned in the previous assessment but to a lesser extent. Moderately cooperative partners often have a stubborn streak, and while they may demand to have their way, they also have an agreeable side that prefers to avoid confrontation. They will often find ways to avoid conflict, preventing disagreements from spiraling out of control. Both partners must learn to compromise and approach intimacy with a give-and-take spirit. Developing effective communication skills and respecting each other's feelings and boundaries will help maintain a healthy balance in this relationship. By working together to identify and address their major points of contention, and by negotiating mutually agreeable compromises, these partners will be able to create a stable, harmonious environment where sexual intimacy can flourish.

Both partners are conventional: These relationships are typically complicated by stubborn obstinance and competition for the upper hand. Disagreements, sometimes fierce, may be common. Neither partner will desire compromise nor budge from their views, leading to a stand-off. Both may hold out for short-term wins, but that eventually exacts a heavy toll on intimacy. Such stubborn entrenchment is less likely—in fact, compatibility could be high—where both partners share the same religion, politics, or strong societal views. This could tilt the outlook for agreeability from difficult to favorable. However, in relationships where the partners' core beliefs fall at opposite ends of the spectrum, compatibility plummets and the risk of significant discord and relationship failure increases exponentially.

Ironically, partners in these difficult relationships may remain together for years, despite intimacy and affection being long gone, because their stubbornness won't allow either of them to admit defeat and move on. Their friends might speculate that they stay together just to make each other miserable. To restore harmony to such a relationship, both partners must yield and compromise, understanding that no partnership can endure without cooperation. By embracing tolerance and adaptability, and rekindling the attraction and love they once felt for each other, there is always hope for revitalizing even the most strained relationship.

A Final Thought

After calculating all five aspects of your Sexual Interaction Profile and perusing the interpretations, you should possess a wealth of insights into the physical side of your relationships and steps for implementing meaningful improvements. As we discussed in the previous chapter on emotional interaction, the insights provided by numerology can be remarkably accurate. But we must not forget that life experiences and day-to-day relationship interactions may alter an individual's feelings, reactions, attitudes, and overall personality. Numerology provides signposts revealing how we might be influenced by the spectrum of universal vibrations if we do nothing to modify their impact. But humans are imbued with free will. Over time, they can learn, change, progress, or take steps backward, and this evolution might not always align with the patterns we find in their numerology chart.

Using numerology to evaluate sexual compatibility gives us a valuable tool that we can use to understand and enrich physical intimacy. It reveals latent and hidden attitudes, desires, habits, and behaviors that mold our sexuality. By gaining a better understanding of these nuances in ourselves and our partners, we can navigate conflicts and differences more efficiently, increase mutual understanding and rapport, and build more vibrant and ultimately satisfying relationships.

Chapter 11
Your Love Forecast

Over the course of history, civilization has undergone a remarkable evolution. We have witnessed cycles of famine, prosperity, war, global pandemics, medical breakthroughs, and transformative revolutions in industry, science, and technology. Just as the ocean's tides change and the moon completes its orbit every twenty-eight days, these events coincide with universal energies that ebb and flow in predictable cycles. In numerology, we refer to these cycles as "cosmic rhythms." And by using numerology, we can study the workings and effects of this natural phenomenon. For instance, we can ascertain which vibrations are influencing the world, or any individual on a personal level, at any particular moment, be it past, present, or future. We can also ascertain the predictable cascade of effects that will occur as these energies ebb and flow.

Have you ever wondered why some days are filled with productivity and progress, while others bring nothing but grief? Why one month favors financial gain, another brings positive developments in romance or career, while yet another would best be spent hiding out at home waiting for the storm to pass? These fluctuations coincide with cosmic rhythms, an ever-changing confluence of universal vibrations continuously at work in our daily affairs. This extraordinary insight underpins the benevolent as well as the adverse trends we encounter from year to year, month to month, and day to day in our journey through life.

Using numerology to identify and analyze your "Personal Rhythm," we can identify the vibrations affecting everything in your life at any particular time in the present, past, or future. Your Personal Rhythm can reveal pitfalls and opportunities that await you in every facet of life, from work to romance to health. With this knowledge, you can discern when to act and be able to circumvent pitfalls, avoid mistakes, seize opportunities, and initiate success-driven decisions that can change your life.

Previously, in Chapter 2, you learned a simple technique for calculating your Romantic Destiny vibration. That same number corresponds to your Personal Rhythm. From that, you can extrapolate a surprisingly accurate numerology forecast for yourself, your partner in romance, or anyone else. In this book, we will focus on crafting numerological love forecasts, but the steps are the same for delving into any area of your life. Just follow the instructions presented in the following pages.

How To Calculate Your Personal Year Vibration

We'll begin with a simple mathematical formula to deduce your Personal Year vibration. This reflects the prevailing influences at work in your life during any particular calendar year.

1) Refer to your basic numerology chart and look up your Romantic Destiny vibration. If you have not yet calculated this value, refer to Chapter 2 and follow the instructions for Step #2.

2) Refer to the Personal Year Conversion Table on the next page and find the current calendar year. The number to the right of the year is the "Cosmic Year" vibration for that year.

3) Add the Cosmic Year number to your Romantic Destiny vibration. Then, reduce the sum to either a primary vibration (1-9), or a master vibration (11, 14, 16, 19, or 22). This is your "Personal Year" vibration for that calendar year.

4) Refer to the interpretations following the conversion table to understand the significance of your Personal Year vibration and how it will affect your life during those 12 months.

Personal Year Conversion Table

Year	#	Year	#	Year	#	Year	#
1920	3	1960	16	2000	2	2040	6
1921	4	1961	8	2001	3	2041	7
1922	14	1962	9	2002	4	2042	8
1923	5	1963	19	2003	5	2043	9
1924	16	1964	2	2004	6	2044	1
1925	8	1965	3	2005	7	2045	11
1926	9	1966	22	2006	8	2046	3
1927	19	1967	5	2007	9	2047	4
1928	2	1968	6	2008	1	2048	14
1929	3	1969	7	2009	11	2049	6
1930	4	1970	8	2010	3	2050	7
1931	14	1971	9	2011	4	2051	8
1932	6	1972	19	2012	5	2052	9
1933	16	1973	2	2013	6	2053	1
1934	8	1974	3	2014	7	2054	11
1935	9	1975	22	2015	8	2055	3
1936	19	1976	5	2016	9	2056	4
1937	2	1977	6	2017	1	2057	14
1938	3	1978	7	2018	11	2058	6
1939	22	1979	8	2019	3	2059	16
1940	14	1980	9	2020	4	2060	8
1941	6	1981	19	2021	5	2061	9
1942	16	1982	2	2022	6	2062	1
1943	8	1983	3	2023	7	2063	11
1944	9	1984	22	2024	8	2064	3
1945	19	1985	5	2025	9	2065	4
1946	2	1986	6	2026	1	2066	14
1947	3	1987	7	2027	11	2067	6
1948	22	1988	8	2028	3	2068	16
1949	5	1989	9	2029	4	2069	8
1950	6	1990	19	2030	5	2070	9
1951	16	1991	2	2031	6	2071	1
1952	8	1992	3	2032	7	2072	11
1953	9	1993	4	2033	8	2073	3
1954	19	1994	5	2034	9	2074	4
1955	2	1995	6	2035	1	2075	14
1956	3	1996	7	2036	11	2076	6
1957	22	1997	8	2037	3	2077	16
1958	5	1998	9	2038	4	2078	8
1959	6	1999	19	2039	14	2079	9

1

New love affairs; new friends and social contacts; new projects and adventures; a focus on initiating plans and goals; sudden, unexpected change, and potential confusion or chaos caused by over-reaction; possible marriage or birth of a child; This year is brimming with opportunities for growth and exploration. It is a time for confidence, action, innovation, and achievement. Welcome the new, be open to change, take risks, and embrace bold plans in love and life. Seize the moment to forge new connections and expand your horizons.

2

Cooperation between friends and loved ones; harmony; optimism; happiness in love; tranquil home life; balanced relationships; empathy and compassion; a diminishing risk of misunderstandings and discord; romances become more harmonious; hope and good cheer prevail. This is a year for nurturing, reconciliation, and strengthening love relationships, friendships, and family ties. Build bridges and open new lines of communication. Plant seeds of harmony and mutual trust. Work to deepen intimacy through encouragement and sensitive interaction, and build trust in your love relationships. By embracing a spirit of cooperation and goodwill, you'll be able to establish harmony and joy in your romances and personal life.

3

Creativity; artistic expression; drama; freedom of thought and action; emotional intensity; new romances form suddenly; brief episodes of moodiness and impulsivity; new friends, popularity, and adventure. This year favors breaking out of routine, meeting new people, broadening life viewpoints, and seeking enjoyment in new experiences. A free spirit, self-expression, and exploration of your creative potential are highlighted. Embrace your passions, and pursue your dreams.

Be open to new ideas and experiences, new relationships, and new ways of viewing love, life, and the world.

4

Hard work; perseverance; accomplishment-driven effort; stable romantic conditions and happiness (for partners who remain grounded); possible tension between extroverted or idealistic lovers as progressive thinking clashes with the traditional; possible boredom, stoked by a year-long cycle of routine and attention to detail; new job responsibilities or advancement. This year, the down-to-earth 4 vibration will require hard work, attention to detail, and persistence. It may be a challenging time for lovers who lack stability or a spirit of cooperation. Focus on building a solid foundation in personal and romantic affairs. Embrace stability, and take practical steps to execute previously laid plans for your success and happiness. Wild ideas, speculation, risk-taking, and unrealistic daydreams are not favored and will lead to wasted effort. Maintain stability and embrace a tolerant approach to love and life to make the most of the practical 4 vibration during this 12-month cycle.

5

Excitement, pleasure, social mingling; travel with intimate partners; relief from burdensome responsibilities, as well as relief from boredom and routine; sudden, intense infatuation; preoccupation with sex; casual relationships; tension at home due to too many outside activities and interests. This year brings freedom, adventure, and relaxation. Embrace new experiences and enjoyable pastimes. Allow yourself to explore and enjoy life to the fullest. However, be mindful of the need to maintain balance and good sense. A stimulating, new love affair could develop suddenly (but situations that may lead to scandal or loss of reputation). Avoid risk-taking and over-indulgence. Keep a close watch on your health this year.

6

Emotional security; optimism; harmony; family and home life; romantic bliss; emotional rather than physical intimacy; quiet times and happy memories; a cooperative approach to relationships; compassion; sensitivity; a new romance could blossom; possible discord over a past lover. Sometimes called "the marriage vibration," the 6 shifts the focus from the 5's cycle of adventure to home life, family, close friends, and love. This cycle is auspicious for marriage and childbirth. It is a time for mending strained relationships and building trust. New responsibilities will arise, perhaps involving an older family member, a youngster, or a partner's health setback or disability. Emotional security, honesty, and open communication are highlighted. Take advantage of opportunities to strengthen emotional bonds and forge deeper intimacy. Find tranquility and joy in secure and emotionally fulfilling relationships.

7

Wisdom; self-awareness; intuition; kindness; sensitivity; analytical thinking; truthfulness and truth-seeking; optimism; empathy; spirituality; but also the potential for pitfalls associated with the 7 vibration to emerge, including hyper-sensitivity, insecurity, impulsivity, pessimism, fear, secrecy, jealousy, and possessiveness. This year will require a thoughtful and balanced approach to everyday life with an emphasis on honesty, balance, clear thinking, and self-control. Those who choose not to embrace these attributes may find this year challenging. Moods and impulses must be controlled. This is a time for analysis, self-reflection, and wisdom. Allocate time for self-care, and avoid conflict. Focus on building trust and rapport in your relationships. Be fair and compassionate. By embracing truthfulness sweetened with empathy, and by strengthening your sense of equilibrium and well-being, you can navigate the challenges of this year and find inner peace.

8

Emphasis on career and advancement; self-improvement; leadership opportunities; financial gain; generosity; heightened charisma; stable home and love life; recognition or acclaim; major projects move forward. The 8 vibration favors material success, leadership, wealth, and power. Those who focus their energies on these endeavors should see their efforts rewarded. This cycle promotes financial growth and career advancement. Expect stability in romance and family. Opportunities will arise to strengthen existing relationships, and the effort will be well rewarded. Traveling with a spouse for business or pleasure may bring happy memories. Now is the time to launch new projects, move existing plans forward, and reap the rewards of past efforts. While this very materialistic cycle prevails, don't lose touch with your spiritual side. Look for the deeper meaning of your success and try to understand how it could enhance other areas of your life.

9

Spirituality; self-analysis; willing service; charity; making amends for past mistakes; tying off loose ends and bringing closure to unfinished business; forgiveness; seeking answers to existential questions about life and destiny. The 9 vibration is often called "the finishing vibration," and when its influence extends to your Personal Year, it brings closure and release from conditions that have been weighing you down. To make the most of this time, tie off loose ends and let go of burdensome responsibilities that should no longer concern you. Focus on self-discovery and spiritual growth. Attend to your physical and emotional well-being, approaching daily life with optimism and patience. Avoid initiating new projects. Take advantage of this 12-month cycle to revamp your emotional landscape and relax, enjoying some quiet time before the 1 vibration returns next year with a fresh infusion of change and new beginnings.

11

Fascination with the new, the unusual, and the exotic; active social life; dramatic expression; success may come from artistic endeavors; a tendency to procrastinate; unpredictable or impulsive behavior; unusually strong interest in love and sex, especially the latter; sudden, deep infatuation; emotional intensity; idealistic goals; new romances, or possibly an illicit affair. This year ushers in a cycle of spontaneity, creative urges, and a yearning for excitement and adventure. There's a strong likelihood that you might embark on an unusual odyssey that will change your outlook on life. You may develop a new (or renewed) fascination with some field of interest that aligns with your worldview, such as philosophy, religion, history, or mysticism. Embrace your passions and explore new modes of self-expression. For instance, this would be a good time to try your hand at writing, painting, or music. Avoid impulsive behavior, and maintain stability in daily living. The allure of new, unconventional, or even provocative sexual experiences may intrigue you, but you'll find greater fulfillment by building deeper intimacy and responsiveness with an exceptional lover who can bring out your best qualities.

14

Adventure; popularity; physical magnetism; increased sex drive; sensuality; new friendships and new love affairs, but not all end well; risk-taking; travel; moderate success in business or career endeavors; for some, possible over-indulgence leading to health concerns; a risk of accidents (for men) and unplanned pregnancy (for women). This year may lead you on a whirlwind of adventure. Colorful new friends and exciting life experiences may be on your horizon. Embrace your charisma and fun-loving zest for life and prepare to explore the world. Be ready to seize opportunities for excitement and pleasure, but practice self-restraint and use discretion. Strive for moderation to avoid over-indulgence, which is a pitfall of the 14 vibration. During this cycle, it's best to refrain from unnecessary risk-taking and invest extra effort into maintaining your health and well-being.

16

Deep emotional feelings; heightened sensitivity; intuitive; perceptive; sympathetic; in search of one's soul mate; sudden infatuation; blurring the lines between love and sex; secrecy; impulsiveness; lack of discretion, or deception; for some, romantic discord or the end of a love affair. This year brings a cycle of unusually intense and erratic emotions, moodiness, and impulsivity, a yearning for soulful, passionate love, and, for some, indiscretions that may have consequences. Pretty much the entire year will revolve around love, the search for it, or its loss. Happiness in romance won't come easy, but it is possible for those who exercise self-control, good judgment, and a grounded approach to intimacy.

The 16 vibration stirs passions and ignites sensuality. However, these qualities are problematic when invested in a passing affair that ends quickly and never had a chance of enduring. It would be better to seek such profound intimacy in an established love affair that can be enhanced and deepened through mutual trust and affection. The volatile, high-stakes nature of romance requires a delicate balance of passion, self-control, and groundedness. Those who can maintain this balance will be more likely to find happiness in love during this Personal Year.

19

A mix of new beginnings and abrupt endings; unexpected change that comes suddenly; new friends appear and old friends depart; unpredictable circumstances which are difficult to control; introspection; psychic awareness; seeking answers to spiritual questions; for some, possible loss of reputation or wealth due to poor judgment. The 19 Personal Year brings unpredictability, and that's a good overview of what to expect during this 12-month cycle. An amalgamation of the 1 vibration, which promotes newness and change, and the 9, which brings closure and endings, the 19 vibration accelerates fresh starts and overdue endings, which now may happen very quickly. Launching new plans is favored, and so is making new plans to be launched at a more auspicious or feasible time. Either way, seize opportunities for success and financial gain as they arise, but at the same time, invest some energy into inner growth and self-awareness. Search for life's deeper meaning. Avoid any temptation to misuse power or authority during this cycle. While it is not a favorable time for initiating new romances, existing love affairs can thrive, so the best use of time and energy this year will be to infuse new intimacy and passion into an established romance.

22

Material gain; career advancement; promotion; self-improvement; education; attention to detail; making plans and putting them in motion; dependability; organization; good judgment. This year favors growth, coordinated efforts with others, and progress. The 22 vibration swings the primary focus to career, job security or promotion, education, and financial security. Accumulation of wealth is favored; also, construction and building. Opportunities for learning a new skill or a trade, or pursuing an education, may arise and should be pursued, as learning and self-improvement are well-aligned with the 22 vibration. In love, strengthen existing bonds or devise a plan with your partner to improve your relationship and deepen intimacy progressively, month by month. Take practical steps to build a solid foundation for enduring happiness. Throughout the year, focus on getting organized or staying that way, and exercise tolerance, open-mindedness, and good judgment in all aspects of life.

How To Calculate Your Personal Month Vibration

In addition to Personal Year trends, other cyclical vibrations can influence your romances and life in general from month to month. Some numerologists regard Personal Month trends as even more important than Personal Year vibrations, but both are equally significant. By tracking Personal Month trends, you can more precisely anticipate and prepare for the effects of universal vibrations over shorter intervals.

To calculate your Personal Month vibration, you must know your Personal Year vibration. If you have not already done so, determine your Personal Year vibration using the method described above, and jot it down.

Look in the Calendar Month Table below to find the number value for the month you want to analyze. For instance, January is 1, February is 2, and so on. For this calculation, we always reduce month numbers to a primary vibration (1-9), as shown in the table, so November is 2, not 11.

CALENDAR MONTH TABLE

January	1	July	7
February	2	August	8
March	3	September	9
April	4	October	1
May	5	November	2
June	6	December	3

Add the calendar month value from the table to your Personal Year number. Reduce the sum to a primary (1-9) or master (11, 14, 16, 19, and 22) vibration to discover your Personal Month vibration for the month you've selected.

To decipher the meaning of your Personal Month vibration and its impact on your romantic relationships and other areas of your life, refer to the interpretations on the following pages.

1

This month brings a whirlwind of unexpected changes and intriguing shifts in your romantic landscape. Whether it's the arrival of a new lover or a transformative leap in an existing relationship, love looms large on the horizon. Boredom will vanish as you encounter myriad opportunities to forge new social and romantic connections. Embrace the exhilaration of unique and unusual life experiences, and don't allow minor setbacks or personal fears to dampen your spirit. Approach each day with enthusiasm, mingle with a diverse crowd, and seize the opportunities for emotional and sexual fulfillment that come your way.

2

Under the influence of the 2 vibration, emotions become the focal point of your life. Love and marriage gain prominence this month. You may find yourself being more affectionate and demonstrative than usual, but bear in mind that you might also be more sensitive. Prevent yourself from falling into sporadic bouts of melancholy or occasional periods of depression, especially if you're naturally prone to insecurity. A cooperative attitude is crucial for fostering harmonious relationships. Welcome the opportunities for intimate fulfillment this vibration offers. Encourage your partner to take the initiative and bring excitement into your relationship. Avoid making major changes or pivotal decisions during this monthly cycle. Instead, relax, go with the flow, and enjoy life as it happens. If the month starts on a sour note, reaching out to an ex-lover could lead to surprising developments.

3

The 3 month favors an artistic and inspired approach to daily living. You'll experience a renewed sense of vitality and find yourself exhibiting dramatic and creative qualities. Your heightened physical magnetism will enhance your social sphere. This vibration brings change and adventure. As the month progresses, the importance of sex may become more prominent. Incorporating provocative encounters or unusual lovemaking techniques into your relationship can unlock new dimensions of pleasure. To fully enjoy this trend, it's crucial to maintain an upbeat mindset but at the same time exercise self-control to safeguard your mental and physical well-being. Break free from routine, embrace bold and sociable characteristics, and be the trendsetter in your social circles. Take the lead as the initiator to elicit a favorable response from your mate or a prospective lover.

4

The tempo of this month is shaped by your actions during the previous month. If you managed to shake off routine and enjoy an active social life, you can now slip into a comfortable and harmonious lifestyle. Relationships begun or carried over from the previous month may intensify and deepen. However, those who failed to escape the mundane may encounter a month-long cycle of tedium. Inactivity and adherence to routine may trigger restlessness and irritability. Resist the urge to act impulsively to break free from the monotony, as the 4 vibration favors honesty, loyalty, and emotional stability as the antidotes to boredom. Concentrate on maintaining stability and invest more time and effort into your job, career, finances, or home improvement during this period. This will better position you to make forward strides in these aspects of day-to-day living.

5

The 5 vibration introduces a rejuvenating and stimulating trend, often bringing provocative life experiences and variety. Glamorous love affairs and adventure take center stage while existing relationships become more casual and trusting. Sex gains importance, particularly toward the middle of the month. The 5 vibration enhances your sex appeal to potential mates and numerous opportunities for intimate fulfillment may surface. Serious involvements are not favored until the final week of the month, but it's best to postpone commitments until next month when the 6 vibration will foster deeper intimacy and enduring relationships. As you embrace the adventurous aspects of this Personal Month trend, exercise moderation to avoid appearing headstrong or hedonistic, which may dissuade new social contacts. Be mindful of the potential for occasional lapses in judgment, and think before you act or make significant decisions regarding affairs of the heart.

6

The 6 vibration, often referred to as the "marriage trend," heightens the focus on love affairs and the establishment of lasting commitments. Family matters and home life gain prominence throughout the month, with romance becoming a primary focus. Marriage, be it within an existing relationship or the possibility of one, may occupy your thoughts. Interference from friends and family may crop up, but it's crucial to follow your heart and do what you believe is right. For those already in a committed relationship or marriage, focus on transforming your bond into the most rewarding and fulfilling love affair possible. Single individuals can anticipate new opportunities for romance around the middle of the month. Moodiness and lack of confidence are the primary pitfalls now and should be diligently controlled.

7

The 7 vibration ushers in a period of insight, cooperation, and reflective contemplation. However, a propensity to be excessively analytical or, on the flip side, overly emotional may emerge throughout the month. This vibration often induces abrupt mood swings, impulsiveness, and a hypercritical disposition, which can disrupt harmony if not checked early on. Moreover, secrecy and illicit affairs, which are pitfalls of this vibration, must be avoided to maintain a tranquil and agreeable home environment.

While the 7's influence might lead to decreased vitality and introversion, there will be ample opportunities for joy with your mate. Those vulnerable to the negative influences of this vibration might find this month emotionally challenging, with tension and disagreements arising from minor issues. To avert potential romantic discord, control your impulsive urges, exercise common sense, and adopt a patient approach to daily hurdles in love and life.

8

Under the materialistic 8 vibration, career and finances take priority. Romance moves to the back burner as the focus shifts to material gain, self-improvement, and advancement. This is an ideal time to direct your energy into endeavors that can yield personal success and financial prosperity. Consider a change in job or status under this vibration, as it could be rewarding in the long term. Embrace a success-driven approach to daily life, and briefly pause your romantic interests. New relationships are not particularly favored under the 8 vibration, but existing romances will remain steady as you focus on pursuing material objectives. Don't underestimate the importance of this month-long trend; your achievements now can enhance your popularity and appeal in the future.

9

The 9 Personal Month can take an unpredictable course. Use this time to address unresolved matters from the previous eight months. It's best to avoid starting major projects and focus instead on tying off loose ends. This period offers a chance to eliminate unpleasant circumstances in your life, such as faltering love affairs and burdensome responsibilities. As a time for introspection, use it to identify areas in your life requiring improvement. Avoid dwelling on past memories, especially unhappy ones. While you might become introverted or less outgoing under the 9 trend, it's normal to pull back from social interactions to focus on important objectives. Allocate time for reflecting on your current situation and future. Maintain an optimistic outlook, and take the necessary steps to bolster your prospects for love and life moving forward.

11

The 11 vibration often signifies a memorable month, for better or worse, depending on your actions. Brace yourself for an influx of unique, unusual, and exotic experiences. This powerful and enigmatic vibration brings a significant level of unpredictability, with the potential for both pleasant surprises and unforeseen setbacks. Your love and sex life may experience dramatic swings throughout the month. Adventure and a thriving social life are within reach, but self-control and moderation are imperative. If you are married, steer clear of illicit affairs; the ensuing scandal could irreparably harm your relationship.

14

The 14 vibration is typically associated with heightened sexuality, risk-taking, and the pursuit of stimulation. However, this Personal Month trend may be less exciting than anticipated due to a tendency for moodiness and irritability. The month could be further complicated by restlessness, indecisiveness, and an aversion to responsibility. The 14 vibration occasionally foreshadows increased stress as well as physical ailments or accidents. Therefore, it is essential that you relax, practice moderation, and take life as it comes. Try to be patient and understanding with loved ones to preserve harmony. While the potential for physical pleasure is heightened by this vibration, exercise self-control and weigh your actions carefully. For further insights into this Personal Month trend, refer to the interpretations for Number 5.

16

The 16 vibration challenges you to maintain clarity during a month fraught with emotional turbulence. Navigating this period requires a grounded perspective and an unwavering commitment to honest communication. Be wary of potential pitfalls and temptations, such as engaging in illicit affairs or mistaking intense emotions for deep love. Exercise discretion and consider the possible consequences before acting on impulsive desires. Cultivate trust, honesty, and transparency with your partner or potential love interests to make the most of this vibration. Despite its challenges, this month also holds the potential for profound growth and transformation in your romantic life. Trust your intuition, honor your emotions, and approach your relationships with authenticity and integrity.

19

The 19 Personal Month intertwines the influences of the 1 and 9 vibrations, creating a potentially exciting but challenging cycle. The 1 vibration represents new beginnings and exciting prospects, while the 9 signifies a phase of closure and reflection. This blend can result in a mixture of excitement and confusion. You'll be drawn to new opportunities and experiences, but you will also feel the need to evaluate past relationships and let go of what no longer aligns with your path. Navigating the 19 trend calls for patience, self-awareness, and faith in your intuition. Try to strike a balance between embracing new experiences and wrapping up loose ends from the past

22

The 22 vibration emphasizes stability and practicality, offering a month of relative tranquility and positive energy. Both physical vitality and material gain are favored during this month-long cycle. You will be in a position to make important decisions and implement changes effortlessly. The first half of the month favors hard work, personal improvement, and attention to pending obligations. However, it is crucial to stay mindful of your loved ones' feelings, as lack of consideration can be a pitfall of the 22 vibration, causing tension or upset feelings. Balance your focus between personal success and nurturing your romantic relationships. Leverage this period to strengthen the foundation of your love life and prioritize the emotional well-being of both you and your partner. A practical and empathetic approach this month can lead to significant progress in your romantic endeavors and life goals.

How To Calculate Your Personal Day Vibration

To decipher the numerological trends at work on a specific day, choose a calendar day that you'd like to analyze and reduce it to a single digit.

Next, reduce your Personal Month to a single digit.

Add the two single-digit numbers you just obtained and reduce the sum to either a primary (1-9) or a master (11, 14, 16, 19, or 22) vibration. This is your Calendar Day vibration.

For example, if you want to find the prevailing vibration in your life on March 18, 2026, and March is an 11 Personal Month for you, do as follows:

1. Reduce the calendar day (18) to a single digit:
   $1 + 8 = 9$

2. Reduce your Personal Month (11) to a single digit:
   $1 + 1 = 2$

3. Add the single-digit calendar day (9) to the single digit representing your Personal Month (2).
   $9 + 2 = 11$

4. Reduce the sum from Step #3 to a primary or master vibration. As 11 is a master vibration, do not reduce.

In this example, the Personal Day vibration is 11.

To interpret any Personal Day vibration, refer to the corresponding Personal Month vibration presented earlier in this chapter and adjust the meaning for a 24-hour day rather than a full month.

Chapter 12
Charting Your Life Cycles

*I*n this chapter, we delve into the concept of Life Cycles in numerology, which is the final major topic explored in this book. Using a simple procedure, you can map out significant chronological phases of your life. You might have noticed how your thoughts, actions, goals, and even your entire lifestyle can pivot—sometimes dramatically—at certain points in your life. You might be committed to pursuing a particular set of goals, only to one day find yourself veering off in a different direction. These shifts or "transitions" naturally occur as you move from one life cycle to the next, starting at birth and occurring every nine years. Each transition brings a new prevailing vibration and its associated conditions that shape your personal rhythm's ebb and flow.

Understanding your life cycles can offer valuable insights to help you navigate current challenges and devise a practical roadmap for future success and happiness. If you can predict when a specific cycle will begin, its potential impacts, and when its dominant trends will be replaced by new vibrations, you can more effectively guide your life toward success and fulfillment. In this chapter, we will discuss techniques you can use to forecast and interpret the effects of each life cycle and anticipate what lies ahead at any stage of your life.

Most people will transition through a total of nine cycles in their lifetime. The first cycle begins at birth, and the ninth concludes at one's passing. Each life cycle spans nine years. An individual who passes away before reaching old age will experience fewer life cycles.

The following table illustrates how life cycles correspond with chronological age:

Age-Based Life Cycle Table

Life Cycle	Age
1	0 – 9
2	10 – 18
3	19 – 27
4	28 – 36
5	37 – 45
6	46 – 54
7	55 – 63
8	64 – 72
9	73+

When analyzing Life Cycle vibrations, keep the following points in mind:

1. A 9-year cycle is strongest during the first and last year, and during the fifth year when the vibration's strength peaks. This applies to both positive and negative trends associated with any vibration.

2. Life Cycle vibrations tend to have a broader impact on our daily lives than Personal Day, Personal Month, and Personal Year vibrations. However, we must consider all these trends collectively and look for stabilizing influences in other aspects of a numerology chart that could counterbalance the potentially negative influences of Life Cycle vibrations.

3. The interpretations presented below aim to provide a foundational understanding of Life Cycle vibrations, focusing

on love and sex for our purposes in this book. As you become more adept at interpreting numerology charts, you will gain a deeper understanding of the nuanced meanings of vibrations and their overarching implications as they apply to life cycles.

How to Chart Your Life Cycle Vibrations

To calculate and interpret your Life Cycle vibrations, you first need to determine your "Life Cycle Operand." This involves a simple math calculation that uses your birth month and birth year. Follow these steps:

1. Reduce your birth month and birth year to single digits.

2. Add the two values you obtained in Step #1 and reduce the sum to a primary vibration (1-9) or a master vibration (11, 14, 16, 19, and 22). This is your Life Cycle Operand.

4. Refer to the *Age-Based Life Cycle Table* on the previous page and select an age range to evaluate. Take note of the Life Cycle number for that age range, shown in the left column. These values range from 1 to 9. So, for ages 19-27, the Life Cycle number is 3.

5. Add the Life Cycle Operand from Step #3 to the Life Cycle number from Step #4. Reduce this to a primary vibration (1-9) or a master vibration (11, 14, 16, 19, and 22). The result indicates your prevailing Life Cycle vibration for that age range.

Here's an example of the procedure just described:

Birth Month: November | 1 + 1 = 2
Birth Year: 1972 | 1 + 9 + 7 + 1 = 18 | 1 + 8 = 9
Life Cycle Operand: 2 + 9 = 11
Life Cycle Factor (age 19-27): 3
Life Cycle vibration: 11 + 3 = 14

Concluding this example, the Life Cycle vibration in effect when you are between 19 and 27 years of age is 14.

To calculate all nine Life Cycle vibrations, you would repeat the above procedure for each cycle, adding the Life Cycle Operand to each Life Cycle number.

For example:

Life Cycle Operand = 11
Cycle 1 (age 0–9) | 1 + 11 = 12 | 1 + 2 = 3
Cycle 2 (age 10–18) | 2 + 11 = 13 | 1 + 3 = 4
Cycle 3 (age 19–27) | 3 + 11 = 14
Cycle 4 (age 28–36) | 4 + 11 = 15 | 1 + 5 = 6
Cycle 5 (age 37–45) | 5 + 11 = 16
Cycle 6 (age 46–54) | 6 + 11 = 17 | 1 + 7 = 8
Cycle 7 (age 55–63) | 7+ 11 = 18 | 1 + 8 = 9
Cycle 8 (age 64–72) | 8 + 11 = 19
Cycle 9 (age 73+) | 9 + 11 = 20 | 2 + 0 = 2

Double-check each calculation to ensure the accuracy of the Life Cycle chart.

To interpret Life Cycle vibrations, refer to the guidelines presented below. These interpretations provide a starting point and offer general insights into how the spectrum of vibrations will influence each life cycle, positively and negatively. They are designed to be stepping stones as your numerology expertise grows. Given their brevity for the purposes of this book, they don't illuminate all intricacies of an individual's life journey. As you delve deeper into numerology and the subtleties of each vibration, you'll be able to form more specific insights and interpret Life Cycle vibrations with greater accuracy and depth.

Remember, the real value of numerology lies in its ability to offer insights into the spectrum of vibrations and their impacts on our lives. The more you understand these patterns, the better equipped you'll be to navigate your path.

GUIDE TO LIFE CYCLE VIBRATIONS

1

Life Cycle 1: Children are typically motivated by the 1 vibration to embark on a youthful journey of dynamic curiosity and exploration, fueled by an insatiable thirst for knowledge. Their interests, hobbies, and friendships are likely to undergo sudden changes, driven by their strong desire for discovery. Parents should cultivate a stable environment that nurtures individuality, and intellectual freedom as well as self-restraint and groundedness. The challenge and opportunity for growth throughout his life cycle will be in striking a balance between the adventurous spirit of these children and the importance of them developing stability and realistic expectations in life.

Life Cycle 2: Adolescents under the influence of the 1 vibration demonstrate a strong desire for independence and exploration. Their quest for individuality and popularity may at times clash with societal norms and family expectations. A heightened desire for approval among peers is often typical as these young individuals journey through this life cycle. To guide them toward a path of self-discovery and growth, parents and mentors should teach the importance of personal boundaries, autonomy, respect for authority, and emotional balance.

Life Cycles 3-7: Adults under the 1 vibration may exhibit a pioneering spirit, strong initiative, and fearless determination. These qualities will pave the way for a flurry of rapid change, and unique life experiences. The 1 vibration strongly favors the pursuit of success and career advancement, with an emphasis on inventiveness and original thinking. The quest for success and recognition, and a yearning for deep romantic connections, will likely form a significant part of their journey. Navigating life's challenges while remaining focused on personal objectives could bring lucrative opportunities for success and recognition during this life cycle.

Life Cycles 8-9: The 1 vibration often rekindles the spirit of exploration and independence in older adults. This could lead to significant and possibly unexpected changes in their lives, including the formation of late-life romances. Some may decide to launch a new business or try to turn a beloved hobby profitable. Others may purchase a new home, possibly in a different country. Cultivating resilience, confidence, and a fierce determination to follow their dreams will allow these individuals to navigate the challenges of aging with grace. As this life cycle progresses, health becomes more important and will likely necessitate lifestyle modifications.

2

Life Cycle 1: Children influenced by the 2 vibration often display a strong inclination toward cooperation and harmony. Friendly and trusting, they will gravitate toward group activities and seek to surround themselves with friends and harmonious interaction. Abounding optimism and a sunny disposition are characteristic of the 2 vibration's influence. Parents can support these children's development by encouraging their cooperative spirit and teaching them conflict management skills, such as active listening, critical thinking, and effective communication. As they grow older, a need to balance their boundless optimism with the realities of conflict and compromise that daily life brings could serve as a significant life lesson during this cycle.

Life Cycle 2: Adolescents influenced by the 2 vibration will be drawn to peaceful, secure environments and harmonious relationships. They are cooperative and trusting, sometimes too trusting. This nine-year cycle will encourage healthy emotional development with a strong emphasis on teamwork, mediation, and consensus-seeking. Later in the cycle, vulnerability to peer pressure increases, and some of these individuals will have intense infatuations, with the potential for one or more to be life-changing. Balancing the desire for harmony with personal values will be a pivotal learning experience as they navigate their sensitive feelings and relationships. Cultivating inner strength and realistic expectations, tempering the inclination to trust everyone, and developing a stronger sense of individuality may be significant lessons during this phase.

Life Cycles 3-7: Adults under the harmonious 2 vibration express a natural inclination toward optimism, cooperation, and goodwill. Life will seem peaceful and relaxed, but powerful undercurrents are subtly at work shaping this nine-year cycle, and for some, this could lead to a significant turning point in their lives. Decisions made now will have long-term effects and influence future trajectories. At the same time, happiness and contentment permeate relationships, paving the way for a peaceful home life. However, a tendency to be overly trusting could bring discord and consequences. Developing healthy skepticism and a more grounded approach to relationships early in this life cycle will benefit these individuals. Open communication about expectations and boundaries is essential to ensure personal needs and integrity aren't compromised in the pursuit of harmony.

Life Cycles 8-9: Older adults influenced by the 2 vibration may experience a deep-seated need to prioritize harmony and cooperation. They may find comfort in a quiet life and the status quo. They may become so contended that they lose track of time or absentmindedly overlook day-to-day responsibilities. This nine-year cycle favors tranquility and satisfaction, fostering harmonious relationships and a peaceful home life. From time to time, these individuals may need to stand firm against being taken for granted or neglected by loved ones. Because the 2 vibration favors a kind, nurturing disposition, over-generosity or trusting the wrong people could become a problem from time to time. These individuals will find happiness and a sense of purpose in their golden years by devoting themselves to activities that involve preserving their legacy, reinforcing family ties, reconnecting with distant friends, and enjoying the rewards of past endeavors.

3

Life Cycle 1: Children influenced by the 3 vibration will experience a surge in creativity and may develop a highly expressive personality. Curious and imaginative, they will be drawn to artistic pursuits. They will derive immense joy from channeling their feelings and energies into creative outlets. A nurturing but structured environment that promotes creativity and self-expression will foster their intellectual and artistic development. Parents and mentors should teach these gifted youngsters self-reliance and balancing techniques such as relaxation and meditation to help them navigate the intense moods and feelings sparked by the 3 vibration. Learning to embrace self-confidence and groundedness while finding effective ways to channel their feelings into creative outlets are valuable lessons they must learn during this phase to pave the way for success and happiness in the next stages of their lives.

Life Cycle 2: Under the 3 vibration's influence, adolescents typically experience an upsurge in creativity and emotional intensity. A blossoming interest in self-expression and artistic pursuits could coincide with uncharacteristic mood swings and impulsivity. This could lead to periods of instability in the home. An overactive imagination may cause these youngsters to embrace unconventional beliefs or an ungrounded approach to daily life, provoking feelings of self-consciousness. They must learn to anchor their emotions in reality and channel their abundant energies into creative endeavors built on a stable, grounded foundation. Tempering lofty hopes and dreams with realistic expectations will help them avoid disappointment. This life cycle will bring numerous opportunities for growth in emotional self-control and relationship management.

Life Cycles 3-7: Adults resonating with the 3 vibration are likely to find themselves awash in creativity and emotional fervor. This life cycle typically brings a significant increase in creative activity. It encourages new romantic engagements and heightened sensuality. Freedom of thought and action becomes a priority. Artistic pursuits undertaken during this cycle may garner public acclaim or material success. However, emotional fulfillment may seem elusive. Balancing emotional needs and creative preoccupations can present a significant challenge but also a prime opportunity for growth during this life cycle.

Life Cycles 8-9: Older adults under the 3 vibration may suddenly embrace a sense of artistic inspiration as this life cycle progresses. They may exhibit a yearning to pursue creative endeavors, especially music, painting, or writing. Opportunities will arise for them to resurrect artistic talents left behind years ago, and there is a strong possibility that these activities could lead to late-life acclaim. Emotional intensity will be on the rise, and sensitivity to criticism could spark disagreements with relatives or friends. At the same time, the 3 vibration favors establishing new friendships and romantic interests. Striking a balance between self-expression and emotional stability could pose a challenge during this phase, but doing so will bring a vibrant social life, romantic harmony, and opportunities to teach or impart life wisdom to younger generations.

4

Life Cycle 1: Children under the 4 vibration exhibit an inclination towards disciplined behavior, routine, and a focused approach to tasks. They enjoy structure, order, and stability. Most are motivated by a strong desire for accomplishment and praise. They are organized, enjoy learning, and view homework as an interesting challenge. However, these children can quite stubborn, and they are quick to anger when a promise made by a parent is broken or plans don't go as expected. Parents should cultivate a balanced environment that encourages freedom of thought and expression but also maintains structure, allowing these children to explore their capabilities while staying grounded. Emphasizing the importance of keeping an open mind and being adaptable to change can be a fundamental lesson during this life cycle.

Life Cycle 2: Adolescents under the 4 vibration have a strong desire for stability and routine. They strive to be honest and dependable, and they expect the same from others. They have a strict sense of how things should be and may show signs of being set in their ways at an early age. In the latter half of this cycle, they may begin to exhibit workaholic tendencies. If they take more than a passing interest in romance, they may forge a very deep relationship that could lead to marriage. They reject promiscuous behavior in their partners as well as themselves. Increased responsibilities in the home may occur under the 4 vibration, and despite feeling overwhelmed, they will toil on, dutifully fulfilling their obligations. Striking a balance between responsibilities and leisure time won't be easy, but they need relaxation for their well-being. Parents and mentors should help them establish this crucial balance if they are unable to do it on their own. Learning to be tolerant, open-minded, and respectful of others' views are key lessons during this phase.

Life Cycles 3-7: Adults influenced by the 4 vibration will value stability, organization, and structure. They know that hard work leads to success, wealth, and recognition, which are essential to their happiness. As a result, many are workaholics. Their focus on their job or career and their determined drive for success will enable them to achieve their material objectives, but it will strain their love relationships, especially with partners who desire a more spontaneous approach. To maintain their romances and their mental health, these individuals need to find a balance between work and relaxation. They must also cultivate a spirit of cooperation, flexibility, and open-mindedness, even when they disagree with others. In today's world, intolerance and narrow-mindedness are not widely accepted, and if an individual is perceived in that light, they could suffer setbacks and missed opportunities in their pursuit of success.

Life Cycles 8-9: Older adults influenced by the 4 vibration may experience a renewed emphasis on stability and structure. They may find comfort in familiar routines and patterns, and gravitate toward activities that provide a sense of order and predictability. Organization, or the lack of it, could play a key role in their daily affairs. Those who are organized may find that their lives run more smoothly, while those who are not organized may find that they feel stressed and overwhelmed. They will likely pursue personal milestones, which might include choices such as retiring, buying a home, forging a late-life romance, or traveling the world. They may also be interested in enhancing their living conditions or dedicating themselves to cherished hobbies or causes. Tempering their approach to daily life with tolerance and empathy can lead to deeper relationships and greater contentment. By overcoming narrow views that some older people embrace based on their experiences, and by expressing open-mindedness and tolerance for others, they can build stronger relationships and create a fulfilling and meaningful life in their later years.

5

Life Cycle 1: Children influenced by the 5 vibration are outgoing, inquisitive, and adventurous. They are curious about the world around them, and they love to explore, especially the outdoors. They are outgoing and sociable, and they will have a wide circle of friends and popularity as they grow up. During the first and last years of this cycle, and during the fifth year when it peaks, there may be an increased tendency for health concerns and accidents, so risk-taking and intensive physical activities such as contact sports are best avoided. Parents of these children should encourage their natural curiosity and love of adventure, as this will help them develop into well-rounded and confident individuals. They also need to learn time management, impulse control, and the important lesson that actions can have consequences.

Life Cycle 2: Adolescents influenced by the 5 vibration are dynamic, socially active, and often preoccupied with popularity. They may be impulsive and risk-takers, which can lead to conflict with parents and other authority figures. A desire for adventure and change may disrupt their home environment. Parents should strike a balance between encouraging their children's spirit of exploration and teaching responsibility, consideration, and commitment. These young individuals also need to learn how to make good decisions and manage their emotions. By learning the nuances of healthy relationships and understanding the consequences of impulsive decisions, which are key lessons under the 5 vibrations, they can evolve into well-rounded and responsible adults.

Life Cycles 3-7: During these years, while the 5 vibration is in ascendance, adults under its influence typically express heightened interest in adventure, new experiences, pleasure, and social interaction. This vibration often brings exciting but often unexpected life changes. Travel opportunities may arise, and these individuals may also exhibit heightened charisma, which may ignite passionate love affairs. Life will encourage these individuals to embrace their love of adventure and freedom, but they must also ensure that their many interests and hectic activities don't disrupt their work or home life. Being mindful of day-to-day responsibilities and fulfilling those expectations is a crucial lesson of this vibration that can have potential consequences for those who disregard it.

Life Cycles 8-9: Many older adults under the 5 vibration may experience an elevated desire for personal freedom, social interaction, and enjoying life to the fullest. This can lead to travel, late-life romances, and a desire to experience new things. While the 5 vibration is ascendant, these individuals might derive great enjoyment from booking a cruise or embarking on an exotic adventure they've always dreamed about. Reflecting on happy memories and sharing the wisdom derived from life experiences with others can be deeply fulfilling.

6

Life Cycle 1: Under the 6 vibration, children often cultivate deep bonds with favorite relatives, and emotional connections thrive. This cycle also favors inner growth, stable home life, a sunny disposition, and an appreciation for responsibility. Children attuned to this vibration are typically respectful, well-behaved, and cooperative. They are quick learners and excel at school. Encouraging their pleasant, empathetic nature while also teaching the importance of positivity, setting healthy boundaries, and fine-tuning relationship skills can benefit them enormously later in life.

Life Cycle 2: The 6 vibration in this life cycle often causes adolescents to prioritize emotional security, love, and family. They typically develop strong, nurturing tendencies and exhibit a quick willingness to help others, even if it means self-sacrifice. They are likely to also show an early interest in charitable work, teaching, nursing, or social work. Parents and mentors should guide these young individuals toward cultivating emotional balance and expressing empathy in healthy ways. Honesty, loyalty, and maintaining a cheerful, optimistic outlook are key lessons of this vibration.

Life Cycles 3-7: During these years, the 6 vibration brings significant life changes. Marriage, childbirth, and parenting are accentuated. Unexpectedly being called upon to provide extended care for an ailing family member could consume significant time and emotional energy. Romance is favored under this vibration, both forging new love affairs and deepening existing relationships. The desire for emotional security is a strong, driving force. Unresolved issues from past relationships could arise, leading to feelings of melancholy or occasional bouts of depression. The importance of forgiveness and open communication becomes crucial during this life cycle. This can be a time of deep personal growth, as individuals learn to balance their own needs with the needs of others.

Life Cycles 8-9: Older adults influenced by the 6 vibration may experience a renewed, often sudden interest in home life, family, and deep intimacy. These individuals are driven by a strong yearning for roots and emotional security that prompts them to seek approval, affection, and acceptance. Navigating this phase will require emotional balance, optimism, and applying the invaluable lessons these individuals have learned throughout their lives. Smoothing out strained relationships with family and friends and staying in touch with important social contacts from the past can provide a source of happiness and comfort throughout this phase.

7

Life Cycle 1: Children influenced by the 7 vibration are often highly sensitive, intuitive, self-aware, and moody. They're deep thinkers and intensely curious, with a strong desire for praise and reassurance. They are prone to impulsiveness, may sometimes jump to hasty conclusions, and can become overwrought when their expectations are not met. Some of these youngsters may lean toward introspection and could become preoccupied with self-analysis, which sometimes veers into pessimism or insecurity. Self-doubt or lack of confidence may develop, either gradually or suddenly, contributing to a negative self-image. Parents and mentors should foster a healthy emotional outlook in these youngsters by teaching them self-confidence, patience, and effective skills to manage their emotions. Encouraging open dialogue about their feelings, and maintaining a stable, nurturing environment in the home, will help ensure that these children begin developing balance, stability, resilience, and inner fortitude early on, despite the potentially destabilizing effects of the 7 vibration during this life phase.

Life Cycle 2: Adolescents under the 7 vibration may find themselves often experiencing emotional instability that can manifest as insecurity, erratic mood swings, melancholy, and impulsive behaviors. Their emotional state may sometimes create tension and discord with other family members. These challenging emotional conditions may also adversely impact their interaction with friends. They may become withdrawn or isolated, or they may become more argumentative or aggressive. During the last four years of the cycle (ages 16 through 19), many of these young individuals may desperately seek to fall in love so they can enjoy the happiness they perceive their friends sharing, but their outlook may be idealistic and unrealistic. They may be drawn to people who are unavailable or who are not good for them. It is important for them to develop their emotional intelligence and learn how to manage their emotions in healthy ways.

Life Cycles 3-7: During these years, the 7 vibration can exacerbate emotional instability for some adults, manifesting as impulsiveness, pessimism, hypersensitivity, moodiness, and even depression. However, when an individual works to turn the 7 into a positive influence, it can bring a period of creativity, insight, and emotional security. The 7 also promotes wisdom, justice, and critical thinking. It can instill a deep appreciation for the beauty of the world and a strong sense of self-awareness. Adults traversing this life cycle can rely on introspection and self-analysis for a roadmap to navigate its pitfalls and challenges. Honest, open dialogue can mitigate the negative fallout often sparked by insecurity and suspicion, replacing those reactions with their counterparts, stability and harmony. Thus, the overarching lesson of this life cycle is to harness the positive energies of the 7 vibration to mitigate and replace the potential negative effects.

Life Cycles 8-9: The 7 vibration can present older adults with both challenge and opportunity. It can be a destabilizing energy, triggering pessimism, moodiness, cynicism, and depression. However, in its positive form, the 7 vibration promotes wisdom, balance, and self-awareness. Those under its influence choose, either consciously or unconsciously, to embrace its positive aspects or negative consequences of this vibration. Those who maintain emotional balance and self-control can enjoy lives of great richness and meaning. Those who succumb to their emotions are likely to struggle with anxiety or depression and might find themselves isolated from friends and family. Developing emotional resilience and patience can help older individuals navigate the emotional turbulence encountered during this cycle. Striving to keep an open dialogue with family and friends will create more harmonious relationships. By cultivating balance, averting depression, and utilizing mindfulness techniques such as meditation to maintain stability and self-control, they can transform this life cycle into a time of reflection and renewal, ensuring their golden years during this phase are truly golden.

8

Life Cycle 1: When influenced by the 8 vibration, children typically are confident, energetic, strong-willed, and intelligent. As their personalities develop, they will become more result-driven and display early signs of leadership potential. This cycle encourages stability and rapid intellectual growth, which will contribute to their future successes. Parents can foster growth by providing these children with ample learning opportunities, teaching them respect for others, and promoting a balance between work and play. This life cycle is usually stable, favoring education and emotional growth, but it can also hold valuable opportunities to learn empathy and humility.

Life Cycle 2: Under the 8 vibration, adolescents typically exhibit strong ambition, competitiveness, a desire for personal betterment, and leadership ability. These qualities may develop suddenly as the 8 vibration takes hold, and the change will be particularly noticeable in youngsters who haven't previously expressed a strong character or leadership potential. This success-oriented vibration favors academic achievement, and youngsters under its sway typically have a wide circle of friends.

One downside to this vibration is that these individuals, eager to prove their abilities, may overcommit and risk burnout. Parents and mentors can assist them by teaching humility, good judgment, fairness, and generosity.

Life Cycles 3-7: The 8 vibration can inspire adults to take a fresh interest in personal improvement, career advancement, material comforts, and financial success. Productivity soars and notable accomplishments come easily during this phase. New romances are not likely to form, but existing relationships flourish. Significant life changes, such as relocating to a new town, making a major career move, or purchasing a new home could unlock new opportunities. Maintaining a balance between work and personal life is crucial to ensure harmony in close relationships during this dynamic and productive period.

Life Cycles 8-9: The 8 vibration may inspire some older adults to channel their energies into personal improvement or money-making efforts. Others may be motivated to contribute their knowledge or skills honed over their lifetime to their extended family or local community. A significant and perhaps unexpected change in their living situation is likely during this life cycle, and relocating cross-country or to another country could pave the way for interesting opportunities to explore in their golden years. Striking a balance between pursuing goals and enjoying leisure time will foster harmony in close relationships. This period brings these individuals the satisfaction of reflecting on a life well-lived, and decisions made during this cycle could significantly influence their legacies.

9

Life Cycle 1: When influenced by the 9 vibration, children usually show signs of deep spirituality and self-reflection. They are likely to be intensely interested in the world around them and may ask questions about profound or existential matters that their parents have difficulty answering. The soul-stirring effects of the 9 vibration can sometimes trigger emotional turbulence, introversion, and moodiness. These youngsters' deep curiosity about the world may lead to a fascination with religion or history, although it may be brief. Parents can nurture their spiritual curiosity while teaching them stress management skills to handle any anxiety or other emotional fallout arising from their heightened sensitivity during this life cycle.

Life Cycle 2: Adolescents under the 9 vibration may express a sudden and rapidly evolving interest in spirituality and self-analysis. They may question societal norms and their place in the world, stirring up anxiety and tension at home. At times, these young individuals may become withdrawn or introspective to such a degree that parents begin to worry. Their philosophical tendencies and inquisitiveness should be nurtured, and parents or mentors can teach mindfulness techniques to help them manage stress or overly sensitive emotions. Encouraging an active social life and healthy interaction with peers, and emphasizing open communication and self-expression, can help these young individuals navigate through complex emotions and relationship instability that often accompanies this vibration.

Life Cycles 3-7: Adults influenced by the 9 vibration often embark on journeys of self-reflection and spiritual exploration. This life cycle typically marks an introspective phase in which existing relationships are reassessed and those that no longer align with their goals are ended. The focus now is on weeding out the old and preparing for the new that will come in the next life cycle. These individuals will often find themselves in situations where they give much of themselves, even though doing so is emotionally draining or physically exhausting. Potential health issues and domestic turbulence may surface, and navigating this trend will require resilience, patience, close attention to health, and strong self-awareness. Wisdom derived from their life experiences will see these individuals through this nine-year phase.

Life Cycles 8-9: Under the influence of the 9 vibration, older adults often find the sudden motivation to embark on a journey of self-analysis or a spiritual quest. They may redefine their relationships and sever outdated connections. The 9, "the finishing vibration," can bring personal challenges and a sense of loneliness as the old is discarded, making way for the new that will come when the next cycle, dominated by the 1, brings novel experiences and change. Despite potential challenges, this nine-year cycle will present many opportunities for inner growth, deeply fulfilling relationships, and tranquility. These individuals can pave the way to happiness and fulfillment by relying on their lifetime of wisdom, maintaining a positive outlook, and seeking support from family and friends when needed.

11

Life Cycle 1: Children influenced by the 11 vibration are usually vibrant and expressive. They are curious and eager to learn, and they have a natural thirst for knowledge. They are also very creative and imaginative, but they can be quite dramatic. They may seem deep, intense, and thoughtful, and their eyes sometimes reflect a wisdom that suggests they are old souls. Some are gifted with psychic abilities and have an uncanny knack for knowing what others are thinking or feeling. Parents can foster their children's love for learning by providing a safe space for self-expression and guiding them to understand their surging emotions. Encouraging responsible decision-making and teaching them that their actions can have consequences also will greatly benefit their emotional growth and lay the foundation for a productive and rewarding life in adulthood.

Life Cycle 2: Under the influence of the 11 vibration, adolescents may be unpredictable and dramatic. They may suddenly change their mind or go off on a tangent. Artistic and imaginative, they often use their creativity to communicate their thoughts and feelings. They are sometimes drawn to drama and the arts. Prone to heightened sensitivity and mood swings, they may struggle to regulate their emotions, and they sometimes act impulsively or without thinking. They may also unpredictably alter their preferences, such as favorite foods or relatives, without apparent rhyme or reason. This can be challenging for parents and caregivers, who may find it difficult to keep up with their changing needs. Parents and caregivers can help their kids navigate this tumultuous period by providing supportive guidance also focused on emotional regulation, responsibility, and understanding the implications of their actions. This may include teaching them coping mechanisms for dealing with difficult emotions, helping them to develop a sense of responsibility, and talking to them about the consequences of their actions.

Life Cycles 3-7: Adults under the influence of the 11 vibration tend to be moody and unpredictable. They typically don't like authority and may not always follow the rules. They are emotionally intense and sometimes act impulsively. They're drawn to new and exciting things but have difficulty staying focused on one thing for too long. They are attracted to colorful, eccentric friends and unconventional perspectives. Impulsivity could lead these individuals into intriguing but potentially difficult love affairs. They tend to fall in love easily but may have difficulty maintaining long-term relationships. To navigate the sometimes stormy seas of the 11 vibration, these individuals must learn to make thoughtful decisions and maintain stability in their relationships. Developing a sense of responsibility and learning healthy coping mechanisms will help adults under the influence of the 11 vibration maintain a grounded perspective. They also need to balance their attraction to novelty with a long-term perspective, which may mean setting realistic expectations and making sure their decisions align with their values.

Life Cycles 8-9: Older adults influenced by the 11 vibration typically display the qualities and attitudes associated with the other life cycles: dramatic self-expression, emotional intensity, deep insight, and unpredictability. Throughout this life cycle, they will have a yearning for unique experiences and always be looking for new ways to challenge themselves. Their often dramatic temperament and emotional intensity can create deep and gratifying connections with romantic partners and friends. They are usually drawn to people who are passionate and unconventional, and they probably have a lot in common with them. However, these individuals may find themselves in situations that are emotionally draining or that test their relationships. They may also find it difficult at times to maintain stability in their lives. Exciting opportunities for travel, a new job offer, or forging meaningful new friendships often arrive unexpectedly. These opportunities can be a source of great joy and fulfillment, but they can also be disruptive. To weather the potential emotional storms that the 11 vibration can bring, they will need to maintain emotional balance. They also may need to learn to pace themselves and set realistic expectations. Most importantly, they also should find healthy ways to manage their emotions such as meditation, relaxation therapy, biofeedback, and other popular self-help methods.

14

Life Cycle 1: Under the 14 vibration, children are typically adventurous and charismatic. They are drawn to the thrill of new experiences, and challenges appeal to them. Friendly and outgoing, and they usually have a wide circle of friends. They are not afraid to take risks, break the rules, or go against the grain, and some have a rebellious streak. These children have a natural curiosity and enjoy learning. However, their self-confidence may fluctuate, and they may require frequent praise and reassurance to stay on track. The volatile energy of the 14 brings with it several significant pitfalls, including a tendency for impulsive decisions and a fascination with taking risks. Parents should encourage their children's adventurous spirit but also teach them the importance of safety and moderation to help these youngsters make wise choices and thrive during this phase.

Life Cycle 2: Adolescents influenced by the 14 vibration are typically free-spirited, adventurous, and charismatic. They are drawn to new experiences, and many exhibit a natural talent for leadership. Sociable and outgoing, these young individuals are popular and have many friends. They value personal freedom. They are unafraid of breaking the rules or going against the grain, and some have a rebellious streak. Their self-confidence can fluctuate, and they are prone to impulsive decisions. Some may confuse love and infatuation, leading to stormy but brief involvements. Unintended pregnancy sometimes occurs under this high-energy vibration. Parents can help their kids develop strong, positive characteristics and navigate around the pitfalls of this vibration by encouraging their adventurous spirit but also setting clear boundaries and expectations. They should teach them the importance of safety and moderation, helping them understand that impulsive actions and risk-taking can have unintended consequences. They should also talk to their children about the potential for romantic relationships in adolescence and help them to understand the difference between love and infatuation. Additionally, to counteract the potentially adverse health effects of the 14, these kids should be encouraged to practice self-care, which includes eating healthy and finding healthy ways to manage stress. Although these adolescents will make mistakes, they learn quickly, and with the right guidance and support, they can grow into confident, successful adults.

Life Cycles 3-7: Adults attuned to the 14 vibration are typically gregarious, fun-loving extroverts. They have charisma and strong leadership abilities. They approach challenges with a pragmatic but shrewd determination that usually brings success in whatever they do. At times., they are inclined to risk-taking and over-indulgence. However, they should moderate this behavior, as the 14 vibration is sometimes associated with accidents and poor health. In romance, they often form intense and often purely physical relationships. These involvements are usually volatile and brief. To deepen their intimacy, they should thoroughly discuss their mutual needs and expectations with their partner before rushing into a commitment. Periods of self-doubt or insecurity can impact these adults, and they should surround themselves with supportive people who can offer reassurance and keep them on track. These natural leaders and innovators have the potential to make a real difference in the world if they successfully navigate the challenges and pitfalls of the 14 vibration during this phase.

Life Cycles 8-9: Older adults under the 14 vibration may experience wanderlust and a strong thirst for adventure. They may feel their zest for life renewed. This can be a wonderful time of life, but they must maintain good judgment and a sense of moderation. Over-indulgence and risk-taking behaviors are potential pitfalls of the 14 vibration and should be avoided. These older adults must be mindful of their health and avoid putting themselves in harm's way. In romance, they often form intense relationships with physical pleasure being a key component. These relationships may be volatile and brief. To deepen the quality of their intimate connections, they should thoroughly discuss their mutual needs and expectations with their partner before rushing into a commitment. With open communication and respect, these individuals can experience deeply fulfilling love relationships under the 14 vibration, but they must find a partner who shares their zest for life and their love of adventure.

16

Life Cycle 1: Children under the 16 vibration are typically sensitive, emotional, and idealistic. They may struggle with impulse control and can be easily hurt by the words or actions of others. They may form deep emotional bonds with their school friends. They may resist change, and even relatively minor developments such as a friend moving away or a vacation being postponed can trigger intense outbursts. In addition to their emotional sensitivity, these youngsters are gifted with keen minds and a deep understanding of fairness and justice. In later life, they may be drawn to careers in counseling, social work, or law. For now, they may struggle with perfectionism and self-doubt. Parents should help these youngsters develop a healthy sense of self-worth and encourage them to use their gifts to help others. Parents can also support these children by fostering an environment that encourages open communication about feelings and by helping them understand the nuances of personal relationships and the inevitability of change. Early lessons in self-control, anger management, and coping skills can be crucial during this life cycle.

Life Cycle 2: Adolescents influenced by the 16 vibration are often acutely sensitive and deeply emotional. They are gifted with keen minds and a deep sense of justice. They may be prone to secrecy and might not be entirely honest when they are confronted with facts they would rather ignore or when they feel threatened by parents or authority figures. These individuals may struggle to distinguish between platonic and romantic feelings. Around the age of 15, when this life cycle peaks, they could suffer a period of emotional confusion or upheaval. Intense infatuations, quickly followed by disillusionment, may occur. Guidance from parents on emotional intelligence, open communication, and developing realistic expectations of people and life can help them navigate this challenging emotional landscape. These individuals may be deeply affected by even minor changes in their lives, and they are susceptible to mood swings and erratic emotions. Parents and mentors can help them by providing a stable and supportive environment, reinforcing their sense of self-worth, and teaching them healthy ways to manage their emotions, while encouraging them to use their abilities and gifts to help others.

Life Cycles 3-7: Adults influenced by the 16 vibration are often deeply sensitive and emotionally reactive. These years can be a highly emotional time, with moods, impulsive behavior, and questionable judgment sparked by the instability commonly associated with the 16 vibration. Interactions with family, friends, lovers, and others become a dominant force during this life cycle. This can also be a creative time, and some acclaim is possible, especially for those inclined to writing or music. However, a tendency towards secrecy or impulsivity, if not checked, can inject sudden upheaval into their romantic affairs. Scandals and illicit affairs are common pitfalls associated with the 16 vibration, so restraint and discretion are essential. Cultivating self-control, confidence, and a practical approach to romance can help mitigate potential difficulties arising under this vibration and foster deeper, more meaningful relationships throughout these years.

Life Cycles 8-9: Older adults may find themselves becoming much more emotional as the 16 vibration takes hold. They may struggle with difficult lessons that they learned years ago, but they are now being retested on, especially in the realm of love. Sudden attractions may lead to intense but short-lived infatuations and abrupt endings. This trend could intensify as this cycle peaks around the fifth year. Guidance from close friends on emotional intelligence, open communication, and developing realistic expectations of people and life will help these individuals navigate their emotions. Self-doubt and lack of confidence may occur under the 16 vibration, and friends can help them weather the storm by providing emotional support and reinforcing their sense of self-worth. Despite the potential turmoil the 16 vibration can bring, deep happiness in love and sexual fulfillment are possible during this life cycle for those who cultivate emotional balance and self-control. These stabilizing qualities will not only help them achieve deeper intimacy in love but enable them to age gracefully, ensuring that their golden years are the most wonderful years of their life.

19

Life Cycle 1: Children influenced by the 19 vibration, which blends the energies of the 1 and 9, are typically independent, curious, intelligent, and fearless, but also emotionally sensitive and deep. They are remarkably aware and may sometimes surprise parents with the depth of their insightful observations. Some of these youngsters can be assertive and demanding, which may present challenges related to power dynamics in their relationships. Sudden, unexpected changes may mark their young years, which might seem destabilizing at the time, but it will become clear as their lives unfold that these experiences provided an early training ground for them to develop resilience and adaptability. Parents can support these youngsters by teaching them important lessons about responsible decision-making, emphasizing kindness, respect, and cooperation. These lessons will be stepping stones to leadership positions and authority later in life. Parents should also provide these children with opportunities to explore their interests and develop their talents. Even the seemingly trivial experiences that occur during this cycle will help lay the groundwork for using personal power and authority fairly, efficiently, and compassionately as adults.

Life Cycle 2: Adolescents influenced by the 19 vibration are often highly independent and assertive. They may struggle with power dynamics, and as they strive for independence, they must also learn to respect others. This life cycle can bring numerous opportunities to demonstrate fairness and compassion as well as the crucial lesson of not abusing the trust and generosity of others. Parents can help these youngsters by teaching them leadership skills and responsible power use. They can also encourage individuality and impart valuable lessons in collaboration and compromise. This will enable these youngsters to navigate the challenges of this life cycle and develop into well-rounded adults who will use the power and authority entrusted to them for good.

Life Cycles 3-7: Adults under the 19 vibration often navigate complex power dynamics in both their personal and professional lives. This vibration can present opportunities and tests of leadership. The challenge for these individuals is to use power and authority for positive and constructive ends without resorting to unethical or harmful methods. They need to resist the temptation to take shortcuts or blame others for their mistakes and unwise decisions, understanding that responsibly fulfilling a leadership role is a key lesson in this life cycle. Striking a balance between honesty and fairness on the one hand, and goal-driven behavior, on the other, is crucial. Once they learn to use power wisely, they can achieve significant personal growth and have a positive impact on others.

Life Cycles 8-9: Older adults influenced by the 19 vibration are likely to find themselves in late-life leadership positions. However, this may be challenging, as they will need to rely on the wisdom and insights they've acquired throughout life to avoid the potential for abuse of power. They must recall lessons about fairness, compassion, and responsible use of authority. The same interplay of complex power dynamics will extend into their professional lives and romantic affairs. In these areas, they must avoid the temptation to resort to other kinds of power abuses, such as manipulation, deception, and the belief that the end justifies the means. With a balanced approach, these individuals will be able to continue learning and growing on a personal level, while deriving immense satisfaction from their leadership roles. Despite the potential complexities that the 19 vibration poses, this life cycle can bring great rewards as well as opportunities for spiritual growth and to have a positive impact on the lives of others.

22

Life Cycle 1: Children who resonate with the 22 vibration demonstrate an early yearning for routine and stability. They usually adopt an honest and trusting approach to family relationships, seeking to maintain harmony. They accept change and adapt to it well, earning kudos from parents who describe these children as delightful, disciplined, sensible, and easy-going. Many youngsters influenced by the grounded energy of the 22 vibration are drawn to subjects that involve logic and order, such as mathematics and science. They may show early signs of interest in social justice and humanitarian causes. It is important to teach these children to balance their practical inclinations with empathy and understanding. They may be tempted to focus on their own needs and goals, but they must learn to consider the needs of others as well. To support the development of their positive attributes, parents should provide rich opportunities for comprehensive learning and personal development, which will give them the skills necessary to build deep and enduring relationships in later life.

Life Cycle 2: Adolescents under the 22 vibration typically exhibit a strong desire for self-betterment and stability. They may exhibit a maturity that seems well beyond their years, and their interests are focused on long-term objectives and practical matters. These young individuals value honesty and stability. Maintaining the status quo appeals to them, and they usually resist change unless they see an absolute need for it. Parents can facilitate their children's growth by providing resources that align with their interests while reminding them to relish their teenage years, as they will only be young once. A key lesson for adolescents during this life cycle is learning to balance their down-to-earth approach with emotional intelligence and empathy, which will enable them to prepare for a productive and successful adult life.

Life Cycles 3-7: Adults influenced by the 22 vibration typically prioritize tangible gains, personal betterment, and stability in their lives. They expect dependability and honesty in their relationships and reciprocate these traits. Even those who typically lean towards impulsivity and impracticality may start to exhibit the grounded and reliable qualities associated with the 22 vibration as this cycle gets underway. Sound judgment, willpower, and open-mindedness become indispensable qualities in their daily lives. These individuals may be drawn to careers or projects that involve the practical application of their skills and knowledge, such as science, medicine, mathematics, or engineering. Patience, thoughtfulness, and the ability to resist temptation are essential qualities for adults during this life cycle. They may need to become more patient and tolerant of others' shortcomings, and they should avoid becoming narrow-minded or stuck in a rut. By learning to navigate the generally manageable pitfalls of this down-to-earth vibration, these individuals will be able to achieve great things, build successful careers, make a positive impact on the world, and create a fulfilling life for themselves.

Life Cycles 8-9: As they age, older adults influenced by the 22 vibration become increasingly focused on stability and security. They may become resistant to change, even when it would make their lives better. This is because they have come to value the comfort and familiarity of the known over the uncertainty of the unknown. However, this does not mean that they are not productive. On the contrary, these individuals may feel a restless need to be doing something useful with their time. They may look for opportunities to put their knowledge and skills to good use, either by improving their local community or helping others in need. In friendship and romance, these older adults take a sensible and down-to-earth approach, valuing loyalty and dependability in their relationships. They may be motivated to strengthen existing relationships and bring closure to past misunderstandings. Overall, these individuals are wise and experienced, with a lot to offer the world. They are reliable and trustworthy, always willing to help others, and their passion for making a difference in the world can enrich not only their lives during their golden years but everyone around them.

Chapter 13
Your Love Life by the Numbers

Congratulations on completing this book! You now have the knowledge and tools you need to use numerology to unlock a deeper understanding of yourself and those around you. This can lead to improved relationships, increased personal fulfillment, and a more meaningful life.

Here are some of the key takeaways from the book:

- Numerology can help you understand your strengths and weaknesses, your potential, and your life cycles.

- It can also help you understand your romantic compatibility and the rhythms of your relationships.

- By using numerology as a guide, you can enrich your relationships, minimize misunderstandings, and restore harmony.

Numerology is a tool that can help you understand your life journey, but it is up to you to create your own destiny. Let numerology be your compass, offering direction when needed but not dictating your path. You are the author of your own story, and numerology is simply a tool to help you better understand the script

I wish you all the best in your journey to happiness, personal growth, and meaningful connections. May your life overflow with joy in the coming months and years.

NUMEROLOGY LOVE CHART

Your Birth Name	Partner's Birth Name
Birthdate (xx/xx/xxxx)	**Birthdate (xx/xx/xxxx)**

Major Aspect	You	Mate	Notes
Love Vibration			
Romantic Destiny			
Sexual Consensus			
Karmic Lessons			
Transcendent Challenge			
Life Cycles	**You**	**Mate**	**Notes**
Cycle 1 (0-9)			
Cycle 2 (10-18)			
Cycle 3 (19-27)			
Cycle 4 (28-36)			
Cycle 5 (37-45)			
Cycle 6 (46-54)			
Cycle 7 (55-63)			
Cycle 8 (64-72)			
Cycle 9 (73+)			

Emotional Interaction Profile

Behavioral Compatibility (Assertive/Passive)		
You	Your Partner	Assessment

Self-Confidence Compatibility (Secure/Insecure)		
You	Your Partner	Assessment

Extroversion Compatibility (Extroverted/Introverted)		
You	Your Partner	Assessment

Reactivity Compatibility (Stable/Impulsive)		
You	Your Partner	Assessment

Agreeableness Compatibility (Cooperative/Stubborn)		
You	Your Partner	Assessment

Sexual Interaction Profile

Behavioral Compatibility (Dominant/Passive)		
You	Your Partner	Assessment

Self-Confidence Compatibility (Uninhibited/Inhibited)		
You	Your Partner	Assessment

Physicality Compatibility (Demonstrative/Reserved)		
You	Your Partner	Assessment

Reactivity Compatibility (Spontaneous/Controlled)		
You	Your Partner	Assessment

Agreeableness Compatibility (Openminded/Conventional)		
You	Your Partner	Assessment

NUMEROLOGY LOVE CHART

Your Birth Name	Partner's Birth Name
Birthdate (xx/xx/xxxx)	**Birthdate (xx/xx/xxxx)**

Major Aspect	You	Mate	Notes
Love Vibration			
Romantic Destiny			
Sexual Consensus			
Karmic Lessons			
Transcendent Challenge			

Life Cycles	You	Mate	Notes
Cycle 1 (0-9)			
Cycle 2 (10-18)			
Cycle 3 (19-27)			
Cycle 4 (28-36)			
Cycle 5 (37-45)			
Cycle 6 (46-54)			
Cycle 7 (55-63)			
Cycle 8 (64-72)			
Cycle 9 (73+)			

Emotional Interaction Profile

Behavioral Compatibility (Assertive/Passive)		
You	Your Partner	Assessment

Self-Confidence Compatibility (Secure/Insecure)		
You	Your Partner	Assessment

Extroversion Compatibility (Extroverted/Introverted)		
You	Your Partner	Assessment

Reactivity Compatibility (Stable/Impulsive)		
You	Your Partner	Assessment

Agreeableness Compatibility (Cooperative/Stubborn)		
You	Your Partner	Assessment

Sexual Interaction Profile

Behavioral Compatibility (Dominant/Passive)		
You	Your Partner	Assessment

Self-Confidence Compatibility (Uninhibited/Inhibited)		
You	Your Partner	Assessment

Physicality Compatibility (Demonstrative/Reserved)		
You	Your Partner	Assessment

Reactivity Compatibility (Spontaneous/Controlled)		
You	Your Partner	Assessment

Agreeableness Compatibility (Openminded/Conventional)		
You	Your Partner	Assessment

NUMEROLOGY LOVE CHART

Your Birth Name	Partner's Birth Name
Birthdate (xx/xx/xxxx)	**Birthdate (xx/xx/xxxx)**

Major Aspect	You	Mate	Notes
Love Vibration			
Romantic Destiny			
Sexual Consensus			
Karmic Lessons			
Transcendent Challenge			

Life Cycles	You	Mate	Notes
Cycle 1 (0-9)			
Cycle 2 (10-18)			
Cycle 3 (19-27)			
Cycle 4 (28-36)			
Cycle 5 (37-45)			
Cycle 6 (46-54)			
Cycle 7 (55-63)			
Cycle 8 (64-72)			
Cycle 9 (73+)			

Emotional Interaction Profile

Behavioral Compatibility (Assertive/Passive)		
You	Your Partner	Assessment

Self-Confidence Compatibility (Secure/Insecure)		
You	Your Partner	Assessment

Extroversion Compatibility (Extroverted/Introverted)		
You	Your Partner	Assessment

Reactivity Compatibility (Stable/Impulsive)		
You	Your Partner	Assessment

Agreeableness Compatibility (Cooperative/Stubborn)		
You	Your Partner	Assessment

Sexual Interaction Profile

Behavioral Compatibility (Dominant/Passive)		
You	Your Partner	Assessment

Self-Confidence Compatibility (Uninhibited/Inhibited)		
You	Your Partner	Assessment

Physicality Compatibility (Demonstrative/Reserved)		
You	Your Partner	Assessment

Reactivity Compatibility (Spontaneous/Controlled)		
You	Your Partner	Assessment

Agreeableness Compatibility (Openminded/Conventional)		
You	Your Partner	Assessment

About the Author

Richard De A'Morelli, a seasoned author and editor with a remarkable career spanning over half a century, is not just a storyteller but a time traveler of sorts. As an 18-year-old, in a very different world that existed decades before the Web and Amazon.com, Richard penned his debut work, *Numerology: The Key to Your Inner Self.* That book became a supermarket bestseller and was translated into four languages. In an era when the echo of typewriter keys was the soundtrack to the creation of literary masterpieces, he went on to publish a dozen books on the mysteries of numerology and parapsychology, creating two more supermarket bestsellers that resonated with readers around the globe—*Psychic Power* and *Numerology for Lovers.*

Now, fifty years later, De A'Morelli is presenting a golden anniversary edition of his third book, *Numerology for Lovers.* This captivating work, written at a time when the publishing world was a vastly different landscape, serves as a testament to his profound journey as an author.

While the years have seen De A'Morelli transition from parapsychology to a bestselling author of books on grammar and writing, the essence of his work remains unchanged—to enlighten and engage readers through compelling prose and thought-provoking themes.

Throughout his career, Richard has held prestigious Executive Editor and Managing Editor positions, also serving on the editorial staff of mega-bestselling author Irving Wallace. His impressive portfolio as an author includes two dozen books, covering a spectrum of genres from self-help to fiction, including the widely acclaimed *Elements of Style 2017,* as well as three novels penned under pseudonyms and over 500 bylined articles. The clarity and accessibility of his writing style, coupled with his profound understanding of the written word's subtleties, have solidified his position as a respected figure in the literary domain.

As you turn the pages of *Numerology for Lovers,* allow yourself to be transported back in time, to an era when Richard De A'Morelli was hard at work on a portable Smith Corona typewriter and just beginning to leave his indelible mark on the literary landscape. Journey with him through this fascinating book, and you'll discover that, much like numbers, Richard's wisdom and insights are timeless.

www.ingramcontent.com/pod-product-compliance
Lightning Source LLC
Chambersburg PA
CBHW060353080526
44583CB00012B/296